THE
DREAM
OF GOD

A Call to Return

Verna J. Dozier

Seabury Books
NEW YORK

TO MY SISTER LOIS
"a ministering angel"

Seabury Books
19 East 34th Street
New York, NY 10016
An imprint of Church Publishing Incorporated

Cover photograph by Bob Kinney. Used by permission.
Cover design: Jennifer Kopec, 2Pug Design

A record of this book is available from the Library of Congress.

ISBN-13: 978-1-64065-488-4 (paperback)
ISBN-13: 978-1-64065-522-5 (hardcover)
ISBN-13: 978-1-64065-489-1 (ebook)

TABLE OF
CONTENTS

FOREWORD

As a writer of faith, I usually disclose at my speaking engagements that I am not a theologian and I am not ordained—it is, I believe, my business to be a layperson. I make that disclosure for two reasons. The first is that I know I tend to speak with a tone of authority, and I don't want to mislead in an arena where ordination and, sometimes, a divinity school degree are markers of credibility. I want people to know that what I'm sharing is not the result of formal theological study: I am merely sharing my experiences of God showing up in my everyday life, and of what I've learned in my ongoing seeking that is the spiritual journey.

The second reason is that, and I believe Verna Dozier would agree with me on this point, there is no "merely" about it. What I'm sharing is an important aspect of our faith, inherently credible, and I want laypeople to recognize that they have equally valid experiences and can connect with God and delve into that connection on the same level—no ordination required.

In fact, all the writings and teachings of Verna, as she preferred to be called, validate the layperson to the point where I see I may be a theologian after all. "I think we are all theologians," she once said. "Any time you make any statement about God, you are a theologian. Some of us don't claim that status because we reserve it for people who have great tomes in libraries. This is a great mistake, I think."[1] The ongoing validation was her genius, and she even made it the focus of her ministry.

Verna wrote *The Dream of God* using her texts from a series of lectures delivered during Advent for her home parish, St. Mark's Episcopal Church in Washington, DC. Though originally published thirty years ago, the book still offers an empowering and relevant vision to revive the church even as she points out its weaknesses. It is a gift that this book remains in print for these days, when we seem splintered by our individual searching. Too easily we have learned to forsake the messiness of in-person engagement for the warm and comforting glow of spirituality on our screens. The COVID-19 pandemic, closing thousands of churches to in-person worship, only hardened the issue.

But Verna's message is clear: there's not just a place for laypeople and their leadership in church—they *are* the church, a living, breathing, questioning entity seeking to live into the dream of God she so aptly describes. "The very essence of God's gift is community," she writes.[2] And it is this realization that can save us from ourselves. We are not alone. We have only to reach out and see how we all share in the dream God holds for us.

Though I never met Verna, I feel close to her. We were both born into Baptist families and became Episcopalians as adults. In her small stature but big and gentle heart, Verna reminds me of my late mother, who was the daughter of a Baptist minister. When it comes to faith, I've always likened my mother to basketball wizards like Earvin "Magic" Johnson—phenomenal talent on the court but subpar as a coach, because what she knew came to her so naturally.

Verna, on the other hand, was a phenomenal teacher. Her thirty-four years in the Washington, DC, public schools informed her instruction of Christian formation and empowering laypeople. From her days of teaching Shakespeare, a favorite, she knew students had to understand and interpret Shakespeare on their own. The teacher doesn't give them the words, nor does she do it for them.

Likewise, Verna did not want laypeople to depend on clergy for their understanding of scripture or the development of their faith. They had become too willing to defer to clergy, too comfortable in abdicating ministry to the institution that the church has become. She urged laypeople to take hold of their authority, the authority of their baptism, and seek out their own active ministries as a form of evangelism modeling God's grace in the world.

And Verna would be the first to let you know that there will always be homework. She noted that laypeople have to take responsibility for their own studies by reading multiple Bible translations, perusing critical resources, and having fearless, searching conversations whenever and wherever they could.[3] They have to let go of thinking they might get something wrong and embrace ambiguity. After all, there really are no right thoughts or right interpretations. But there are plenty of questions—and that's okay.

Any reader of The Dream of God may feel the heat of a nearby fire. The prophet's voice is at work in its pages along with a touch of impatience. It's as though Verna, her many years upon her, sensed she had spent too long teaching while too few understood what she was talking about—Don't you see how amazing you are? Like the Trappist monk Thomas Merton, Verna wanted to illumine how people are walking around, shining like the sun.

"God has paid us the high compliment of calling us to be coworkers with our Creator," she writes, "a compliment so awesome that we have fled from it and taken refuge in the church. God does not need such an institution. 'Destroy this temple,' Jesus said, 'and I will rebuild it in three days.' The institution is replaceable. The living body of God's people is not."[4]

The theology in this book is a freedom theology. Here is Verna setting God's people free to answer a call of ministry that is more open, more daring, more compassionate, and, already, so very much our own. Will we be brave enough, faithful enough, to live such freedom? Can we shine the light that God has dreamed into us? That is the life of the layperson. That is, as Verna says, "being about God's business."[5]

> —Sophfronia Scott
> founding director of Alma College's
> MFA in Creative Writing and author of
> *The Seeker and the Monk: Everyday
> Conversations with Thomas Merton*
> April 2021

1. Jay Cormier, "Verna Dozier and 'The Dream of God,'" Episcopal News Service, May 13, 1992. *https://episcopalarchives.org/cgi-bin/ENS/ENSpress_release.pl?pr_number=92117*.
2. Verna J. Dozier, *The Dream of God: A Call to Return* (New York: Church Publishing, 2006), 45.
3. Fredrica Harris Thompsett, "Christian Educators of the 20th Century: Verna Josephine Dozier," Biola University, online resource. *https://www.biola.edu/talbot/ce20/database/verna-josephine-dozier#bio*.
4. Dozier, *The Dream of God*, 111.
5. Ibid., 109.

ACKNOWLEDGMENTS

The ideas in this book crystallized in lectures I was asked by Buzz March to give for the annual Advent Lecture Series for my parish, St. Mark's of Capitol Hill, Washington, D. C. Ray Hartzen videotaped the lectures, while Michael Hopkins, Louise Lowe, and Bart Lloyd read the transcripts and made valuable suggestions in response to my desire to turn the lectures into a book. Susan and Raymond Rich gave generously of their time, resources, and computer skills to prepare the manuscript for the journey to publication under the steady guidance of Cynthia Shattuck, whom I consider a gifted editor and claim as a friend.

I consider myself "wealthy in my friends." I wish I could name all whose faithful interest and loving support sustained me in this enterprise. I thank Dee and Al Hahn Rollins, Jan Hoffman, Randall Day, and Loren Mead of the Alban Institute in the name of them all.

Chapter One

THE DREAM
OF GOD

See, I have set you this day over nations
  and over kingdoms,
to pluck up and to break down,
to destroy and to overthrow,
to build and to plant. (Jeremiah 1:10)

Gracious Father, we pray for thy holy Catholic Church.
Fill it with all truth, in all truth with all peace. Where it is
corrupt, purify it; where it is in error, direct it; where in
any thing it is amiss, reform it. Where it is right, strength-
en it; where it is in want, provide for it; where it is divided, reunite it; for the sake of Jesus Christ thy Son our
Savior. (The Book of Common Prayer, 816)

W hat is your book going to be about?" I was asked
   by a very intelligent and learned man whose
knowledge and skill were sought after by universities on
both sides of the Atlantic, and much valued as well in
the councils and committees of his denomination.

"It's going to be about how I think the institutional church has missed the mark of what it ought to be about," I replied.

"The institutional church?" he puzzled. "What other church is there?"

"The people of God," I replied. "The baptized community."

"But how would they function without an institution?" he smiled.

Aye, there's the rub, as Hamlet would say. The little band, the church of St. Paul's day, needed an organization, a structure, an institution to maintain itself but the institution took over the little band. As Hendrik Kraemer wrote in A Theology of the Laity, most of us tend to think of the church in terms of ministers and clergy, not the people of God.

The prayer with which I began is a prayer for the church as *institution*, and the genius of this prayer for me is that it knows all is not right with the institution. The church can be corrupt. It can be in error. It can be amiss. Institutions, however, do not take kindly to having those possibilities pointed out!

Jeremiah's call to root out, pull down, destroy, and throw down is an awesome call. It can only be undertaken in the light of the complete call—to build and to plant.

The only reason for me to write a book about how the church has failed to be what it is called to be is to hold up again the vision of what it is called to be in the biblical story—the dream of God. The institution has missed its high calling because we the people have missed ours. This book is really about how the people of God have missed the mark, and the institution is only the starting point.

I believe that Jesus of Nazareth is the Messiah, he by whom the reign of God has been made known—and he whom the institutional church, from the resurrection community to the present day, has rejected since the day of his death in favor of something more reasonable, more controlled and more controllable, more human. In other words, I believe Christianity has journeyed far from what Jesus of Nazareth was about.

Of course I am not the first to think that, but my thesis is drawn from what I believe the biblical message to be: God calls a people to be the new thing in the world— the people of God. The new dispensation, the "people of the Way," as the first Christians were called, has missed its high calling even as did the first dispensation, the people of the Torah. The proof of that argument rests with what the church, the institution, has done to the ministry of the laity. The people of the Torah made the gracious gift of the law into a system. The people of the resurrection made the incomprehensible gift of grace into a structure.

Both the people of the Torah and the people of the resurrection were escaping from God's awesome invitation to be something new in the world. I think God was always offering the possibility of living in the kingdom of God in the midst of the kingdoms of this world. Each time the frighteningly free gift of God to be the new thing in the world—a witness that all of life could be different for everybody—this gift was harnessed by an institution that established a hierarchy of those who "know" above the great mass of those who must be told. Each time the world where people lived and worked and had families and friends and wrestled with day-to-day decisions—this world was out of the sight of the holy places. A veil was in the Temple; a rood screen in the cathedrals.

It will take me some time to develop that idea, to trace what I believe is the sorry journey of the people of God from Us to Me, the privatization of religion, a movement away from the dream of God. First, we need to consider what I call the dream of God, what the biblical story is about. Second, we need to think about the rejection of that dream, the three falls. (Of course, human beings are falling all the time, but these three falls are, as I see them, the great symbolic acts.)

What I see as the first fall—what we have termed *the* Fall—is the moment recounted in Genesis when the First Man and the First Woman, Adam and Eve, chose to live another way than the way God had planned for them. That characteristic of any "fall"—the choice against God, the choice for the way of the world—is clearly evident in what I call the second fall, the choice of the children of Israel to have a dynasty of kings like the other nations, instead of what seemed to the people to be God's quixotic system of judges over Israel.

Perhaps because we are so involved in its legacy, my identification of the third fall will seem more ambiguous, but I see the choice for the emperor Constantine as a choice against the uncertainty, the freedom, and the risk of trusting God. God calls us to trust God. These three paradigms witness to our human refusal to live as God calls us to live, and the fall is a theological term expressing that existential reality.

Third, we will look at the institutionalization of this rejection in the church and, fourth, we will see the persistence of God's dream in the call to ministry. I define ministry as service in response to the dream of God, the restoration of the good creation that God brought into being at the beginning and that "groans in travail," as Paul put it, for the people of God to wake up to the reason why they are called.

Christians are not the first chosen people to lose the way. I think that is what the biblical story is all about— the people of God losing the way and a God who will not give up calling them back. Again and again God calls us to return. I think the calling still goes on today, but I believe the Christian church has distorted the call, narrowed it from a call to transform the world to a call to save the souls of individuals who hear and heed a specific message, narrowed it from a present possibility to a future fulfillment.

There was a time when the call was clearly heard—the memory of the covenant in the wilderness.

> Hear, O Israel: the LORD our God is one LORD; and you shall love the LORD your God with all your heart, and with all your soul, and with all your might.... You shall have no other gods before me.... You shall love your neighbor as yourself.

The ancient Hebrews, during the time of their establishment as a nation among other nations, distorted the call by turning it into law. The Christians, during the time of their becoming a structure among other structures of the world, distorted the call by turning it into institution.

But I am already ahead of the story.

This term "story" is important to me, because it says something about how I read scripture. The Anglican collect for Bible study, which in the liturgical calendar comes close to the end of the season after Pentecost, speaks very eloquently of the church's approach to Bible study:

> Blessed Lord, who caused all holy Scriptures to be written for our learning: Grant us so to hear them, read, mark, learn, and inwardly digest them, that we may embrace and ever hold fast the blessed hope of everlast-

ing life, which you have given us in our Savior Jesus
Christ.

First, the collect says God *caused* the scriptures to be
written; it does not say God wrote them. Therefore, God
will not be destroyed if learned scholars find that the
word Isaiah used for "virgin" when he was warning King
Ahaz against finding security in military alliances meant
only "young woman" (Isaiah 9:14), or if they find that
many of those red letters in certain editions of the Bible
were not spoken by Jesus at all, but are instead the words
of the early church.

God did not write the scriptures; human beings wrote
the scriptures. But the faith expressed by the collect is
that God caused them to be written for our *learning*. I
find that word exciting beyond the telling—what a word
to choose! Not for our inspiration. They may inspire, but
that is not the purpose as the distinguished Anglican
who wrote the collect saw it. Not for our guidance. We
may find guidance there, but that is not the purpose of
their being written. Not for our comfort, although we may
be comforted and strengthened by the sacred history.

They are written for our *learning*. There is something
we need to learn, and the only place we can find the subject matter for that learning is in the Bible. We need to
know the story, the story the Bible—and only the
Bible—tells.

The climax of the story is Jesus Christ, the collect
says. And who is Jesus Christ?

In the mysterious and compelling Fourth Gospel,
John the evangelist calls Jesus "the Word made flesh."
What does he mean by that? I think he is referring to a
poem of Second Isaiah, in which Isaiah has God say:

> So shall my word be that goes forth from my mouth;
>   it shall not return to me empty,
> but it shall accomplish that which I purpose,

and prosper in the thing for which I sent it.
(Isaiah 55:11)

The word of God is an image for the action of God, and that verse, very freely paraphrased, says, God will accomplish what God has set out to do. I think the story the Bible tells is about the activity of God to accomplish God's purposes. You will never understand the answer to the question of who Jesus is until you know the story the Bible tells. And that story is not immediately available.

In the first place, the story is not easy to comprehend. The collect suggests much activity has to go into knowing it—hearing, reading, marking, learning, inwardly digesting. It is the work of a lifetime, a study that never ends.

The Bible is not a book; that very name is a misnomer. It is a library of sixty-six books and it is arranged like a library into law books, the Torah, followed by history books, then literature—hymns and poetry and drama and aphorisms and philosophy—then prophetic works. The New Testament has a similar arrangement: gospels, then history, letters, and finally an apocalypse. Obviously reading the Bible straight through from Genesis to Revelation makes no sense, any more than it would make sense to read all the books in the library beginning at the front door.

Nor does it make any sense to read individual books with no reference to the situation out of which they came and to which they were addressed. For example, to read the prophetic books out of the context of the history books is as if you were reading the editorial pages with no reference to the news pages of the daily paper.

The eighth century was a very turbulent time in Jewish history, and the prophets were right in the midst of it. They were reading the signs of the times in the light of what they understood as God's ancient call to God's people. Hear Isaiah:

Woe to those who go down to Egypt for help
    and rely on horses,
who trust in chariots because they are many
    and in horsemen because they are very strong,
but do not look to the Holy One of Israel
    or consult the LORD! (Isaiah 31:1)

This is a statesman (Isaiah) counseling a king (Hezekiah) against a dubious alliance, and 2 Kings 18 and 19 will suggest what was on the front page when these words appeared on the editorial pages of the *Judean Chronicle*.

As a part of the celebration of the completion of the Washington Cathedral, the cathedral staff sponsored a symposium on the story of creation as seen by the scientists and by the Bible. The keynoters were a learned astronomer and an Old Testament scholar, who saw no need to argue about which view was right. The Old Testament scholar Walter Brueggemann began his workshop by saying that the first chapter of Genesis was written during the sixth century B.C.E., the time of the exile. To a people whose whole world had fallen apart, the poet said, there is something, someone, on whom you can depend. A dependable world has been created by a dependable God. The God who delivered them from slavery and sustained them in the wilderness will be with them in exile. They can sing the Lord's song in a strange land.

How can we make sense out of the Bible? It is not easy, and we can never do it by reading any part of it out of the context of the whole story. I believe, however, that making sense of the Bible is essential to the religious enterprise in which we are all engaged.

If we want to know this story that is not immediately available to us, I think we must approach the Bible as we would a great painting. First we stand back and see the painting as a whole, and then we study the details, because however great the details, they are not the painting. If we spent all our time examining the adorable, mischievous cherubs at the bottom of Raphael's great painting the *Sistine Madonna*, we would miss the soaring image of the world's most sublime mother. Similarly, if we spent all our time focusing on the bright gentlemen in the foreground of Rembrandt's painting *The Night Watch*, we would miss the somber bustle of the guard in the background that lets us know who the gentlemen in the foreground are.

A word is needed here about how I approach the Bible before I tell you how I have come to understand and tell the story.

The ancient Israelites were a people of cultic memory, and in song and story and liturgy they kept that memory fresh. It was their memory of special events that had shaped them—the story of a nomad ancestor to whom God had given a great promise, deliverance from slavery, preservation in the wilderness, conquest of a new homeland. The memory included the interpretation of these events that God was acting out for them, that they had a special place in God's plan. Their scriptures kept alive for them the story of who they were.

In the sixth chapter of Deuteronomy we catch a glimpse of how the Israelites used the scriptures.

> Hear, O Israel: The LORD our God is one LORD; and you shall love the LORD your God with all your heart, and with all your soul, and with all your might. And these words which I command you this day shall be upon your heart; and you shall teach them diligently to your children, and shall talk of them when you sit in your house, and when you walk by the way, and when you lie down, and when you rise....

> When your son asks you in time to come, "What is the meaning of the testimonies and the statutes and the ordinances which the LORD our God has commanded you?" then shall you say to your son, "We were Pharaoh's slaves in Egypt; and the LORD brought us out of Egypt with a mighty hand.... And the LORD commanded us to do all these statutes, to fear the LORD our God, for our good always, that he might preserve us alive, as at this day." (Deuteronomy 6:4–7, 20–21, 24)

The Hebrews began with the big picture—faith in a God who acted on their behalf. That is very different from the way we use the biblical record today. I recall a time I was a part of a small group of women who were studying the gospel according to Matthew, the liturgical gospel for that year. We were working with the story of Jesus walking on the water in Matthew 14. The evangelist puts the incident of the feeding of the five thousand before this story. Then Jesus tells the disciples to get into a boat and go before him to the other side while he stays to disperse the crowd. Then he goes off by himself to pray. By the time he is ready to join his disciples, it is late at night and a storm has come up.

In the early morning hours, the disciples are battling the winds and they look up and see Jesus walking on the water toward them. They are terrified, thinking they are seeing a ghost, but he reassures them. Peter cries out, "Lord, if it is you, bid me come to you on the water," and Jesus replies, "Come." Peter starts out and actually walks on the water, but the wind frightens him and as he begins to sink, he calls out, "Lord, save me!" Jesus immediately reaches out his hand and saves him, chiding him for his lack of faith. When Peter and Jesus are in the boat, the wind ceases and the disciples worship Jesus.

Looking up the same story in the other gospels, we found many differences, although only the incident of walking on the water concerned us. Matthew also differs from Mark in that Matthew has the disciples worship Jesus, while Mark (6:52) says they missed the point. Only Matthew includes the incident of Peter trying to imitate the Master and failing miserably. Luke does not have the story at all, and John suggests that the boat was nearer land and Jesus may have been walking *beside* the water. One of the women cried out in desperation, "Which one is right?"

I think she was trying to make sense of a detail before she had grasped the whole picture. A more productive line of inquiry might have been to keep in mind Matthew's whole picture of Jesus and then ask, How does this story fit into Matthew's picture? What is Matthew saying about Jesus with this story? How are the evangelists using the tradition to say what they want to say about Jesus? How do they help us say what we want to say? I do not believe the categories of right and wrong are helpful in approaching scripture because I do not think scripture came out of that way of looking at the world.

I had a friend who, whenever she was confronted with an either-or situation, always said, "There must be a third possibility." I think we can approach the Bible with that third possibility.

The Bible is the testimony of two worshiping communities, Hebrew and Christian, about their faith. It speaks most profoundly to us as we step into that faith view of reality. The opposite of faith is not doubt, but fear. Faith implies risk. I will cast my life on this possibility that God is for me. I do not have to have any proof except my commitment. I do not have to claim complete understanding—that is idolatry. The faith view of reality is frightening in its openness, and so institutions are always trying to control reality with dictums and laws and creeds.

Stories are too fanciful for the timid. They can say too many things at the same time.

The Bible contains history. The history of these two worshiping communities can be traced in its pages—the Hebrew people and the Christian people. It is a religious history, but the genius of the Judeo-Christian tradition is that it is an historical religion. Secular history also knows about Moses and David, Jesus and Paul. Archeological finds continually confirm the factual basis of the biblical story, and it gives worshippers great comfort and excitement to go to the Holy Land and actually walk where Jesus walked, follow in the footsteps of St. Paul, stand on Mount Sinai, and bathe in the River Jordan. This can be carried too far, however, when the dead hand of tradition kills the new thing that God is always doing. An extreme case of this was the Inquisition forcing Galileo to deny what his searching mind had discovered because the book of Joshua had a different understanding. The Bible contains history, but it is also much, much more than history.

The Bible contains literature. The book of Job is one of the world's great dramas, poems abound in the Song of Solomon and in the prophetic writings, and the book of Psalms is a classic hymn book. Short stories (Jonah), novelettes (Ruth), and letters (Paul's epistles) can also be found within the pages of the Bible. The popularity and frequency of publications of versions of the Bible as literature are eloquent witness to this dimension. The Bible contains literature, but the Bible is more, much more, than literature.

For me the Bible is primarily a theological record. Theology is making meaning, making sense out of our lives in terms of what we believe to be the nature of ultimate reality. I always like to illustrate this truth by a story suggested by a friend of mine. He said, "Can you imagine what story would have been told by the lone Egyptian who escaped from the Red Sea debacle? He would have reported to Pharaoh: 'Pharaoh, O King, we didn't plan that expedition very well. We should have been able to calculate the tides better and to have planned our pursuit more expeditiously. Also we should have known that wooden chariot wheels would bog down in that mud. We didn't plan very well.'"

But Moses and the children of Israel sang this song:

> I will sing to the LORD,
>   for he has triumphed gloriously;
>   the horse and his rider he has thrown into the sea.
> The LORD is my strength and my song,
>   and he has become my salvation;
>   this is my God, and I will praise him. . . .
> Thou hast led in thy steadfast love
>   the people whom thou hast redeemed,
> thou hast guided them by thy strength
>   to thy holy abode. (Exodus 15:1–2, 13)

Moses and the Egyptian warrior were dealing with the same set of facts. Slaves were escaping by way of the Reed Sea. Mounted soldiers were following them. The slaves got over to dry land; the pursuers were drowned. For the soldier, the facts had to do with human planning or lack thereof; for the Hebrews, the divine plan was being worked out and they were part of it.

The Israelites made a faith statement. God was for them, and in the power of that faith a people was born, a covenant was established, and we are their spiritual descendants. We, too, look at the world and ask what God is doing, which is another way of asking the question of meaning, the theological question. That is the only question to apply to the Bible, I believe, because it is in answer to that question that the Bible came into being. Is there a God? Is God for us? How can we know God? Does history have purpose?

The most profound theological answer to the question of meaning is God. When we bogged down in the "age of anxiety," it was because God as *the* meaning had lost meaning for us, and the courage of the religious existentialists from Kierkegaard to Altizer was the courage to face existence without God. What the existentialists were really fighting against, as Jesus had done before them, was what the religionists had done to God. What they found out was that it took courage to have faith, that the most courageous statement in the world, perhaps, is the one that begins the Hebrew Bible, "In the beginning God...." By that statement the Hebrews said they would stake their lives on the fact that there is an ultimate reality in the world. Then they went on to be even more daring and said, "In the beginning God created...." Not only is there an ultimate reality in the world, that reality is for us. Creation is an act of love. The ancient Hebrew poet of Genesis, I believe, anticipated the writer of the epistle.

If the creationists only understood that the poet of the first chapter of Genesis is talking about something completely out of the purview of Darwin and all the scientists! He is talking not about *how* the world came into being, but *why*, not about *methods* but *meaning*. The world was brought into being because it is of the very nature of Love to pour itself out in creativity, creative forms, creative relationships.

The God of creation needed to be in relationship to be fulfilled. Unlike other religions, the Hebrews dared the paradox of vulnerable perfection, incomplete completeness. God needed God's creation.

Because we really worship our understanding and because that paradox cannot be understood, our theologians have rushed to make the transrational rational, to make prose out of poetry. Yet theology has to be in the language of poetry because no other language can contain the extravagance of the idea. To paraphrase the philosopher Pascal, faith has reasons of which reason has no knowledge. In Christopher Fry's saucy play *The Lady's Not for Burning*, the woman declares:

> My father broke on the wheel of a dream; he was lost in
> a search. And so, for me, the actual! What I touch,
> what I see, what I know: the essential fact.

And her lively, outrageous companion promptly replies:

> In other words, the bare untruth.

Biblical faith posits a God it cannot understand completely. The prophet Isaiah understood this fact.

> For my thoughts are not your thoughts,
>   neither are your ways my ways,
>   says the LORD.
> For as the heavens are higher than the earth,
>   so are my ways higher than your ways,
> and my thoughts than your thoughts. (Isaiah 55:8–9)

Human beings have always had trouble with this idea.

The feisty protagonist of the Scopes trial said, "God created man in His image and man returned the compliment." That is not the God of biblical faith, but the God of civil religion, the religion we invent to support our nation, our form of government, our way of life. The God of the Bible is both for us and over against us. To lose either side of that paradox in the service of what we can understand, "the bare untruth," is to miss the God of the Hebrew-Christian faith.

When the high hopes of the Davidic kingdom were laid waste by the raging forces of Babylon, the Hebrew people did not say, "Well, we made a mistake. Our God was not powerful enough to bring off his dream." That is what any other people in the world at that time would have said, because defeat of a nation was the defeat of a nation's god. But that was not the Hebrew response, and the human spirit leaped forward light years on their theology.

The prophet Ezekiel was a priest who witnessed the death of Josiah and the ensuing spiritual and political decline of Judah in the sixth century, culminating in the calamity of the destruction of the Temple and the people exiled to a pagan land. He saw that Israel was responsible for her fate, the wrath of God visited upon her for wanton disregard of the vocation for which she had been chosen, a holy people glorifying God. But when the inevitable destruction came, Ezekiel had another word.

> The hand of the LORD was upon me, and he brought me out by the Spirit of the LORD, and set me down in the midst of the valley; it was full of bones. And...behold, there were very many upon the valley; and lo, they were very dry. And he said to me, "Son of man, can these bones live?" And I answered, "O Lord GOD, thou knowest." Again he said to me, "Prophesy to these bones, and say to them, O dry bones, hear the word of the LORD. Thus says the Lord GOD to these bones: Behold, I will cause breath to enter you, and you shall live....And you shall know that I am the LORD." (Ezekiel 37:1–6)

Ezekiel's is a highly poetic theology that puts together the events of history and an understanding of ultimate reality. It bears witness to the fact that God is not defeated by the wretchedness of human beings and can use even that wretchedness to work out glorious purposes. That is the biblical faith. To understand the Bible as a theological book, making sense out of history in terms of an understanding of ultimate reality, it must be seen as a broad canvas.

In the fifteenth chapter of 1 Samuel is preserved an ancient story about the importance of discerning the will of God. Samuel gives King Saul a task. He is to hunt down a troublesome enemy of Israel, the Amalekites, and destroy all their possessions. Saul wipes them out, but decides to spare King Agag and the best of the herds. Then the Lord tells Samuel he is sorry he ever made Saul king, because Saul has not obeyed the Lord's commandments. Samuel descends on Saul in fury, and Saul blithely tells him he has done what Samuel ordered. Samuel wants to know why he hears the bleating of sheep and the lowing of cattle. "Oh, that," Saul replies. "The people spared the best of the sheep and oxen to sacrifice to your God, but all the rest we have utterly destroyed." "Stop!" Samuel shouts. "I will tell you what the Lord said to me tonight." "Say on," Saul answers calmly.

Samuel reminds Saul that God has exalted him from a very lowly place and has given him an order to destroy the Amalekites completely. "Why did you swoop on the spoil and do what was evil in the sight of the Lord?" Saul maintains his innocence. "I have obeyed the voice of the Lord," he declares. "I have gone on the mission on which the Lord sent me, and I have utterly destroyed the Amalekites. But the people took the best of the spoil to sacrifice to the Lord your God in Gilgal." Samuel responds:

> Has the LORD as great delight in burnt offerings
>   and sacrifices,
>   as in obeying the voice of the LORD?
> Behold, to obey is better than sacrifice.
>
> (1 Samuel 15:22)

On casual reading, it may seem that the crusty old prophet Samuel was a more brutal man than the fastidious King Saul, who did not destroy everything of the Amalekites but kept out the best as an offering to God.

Yet Samuel's sharp cry gives the meaning the writer saw in the incident: "To obey is better than sacrifice!" Israel's faith understood that religion can be a pious excuse for subverting the will of God, an understanding that many years later was to be ringingly clear in the prophet Amos.

During a period of peace and prosperity for Israel, Amos was a country boy who came to the big city and was appalled by what he saw. A part of the people of God lived in dire poverty while others luxuriated in shameless wealth. A system of justice open to all had been perverted, while the rites of religion had become a mockery, an outward show of piety. Standing in the most public of places, he castigated the people:

> I hate, I despise your feasts,
> and I take no delight in your solemn assemblies....
> I will not accept them. (Amos 5:21–22)

Because the Bible is a theological book, it is a book of wrestlings, not a book of answers. In each age the people have to struggle to hear the word of the Lord for their time, and sometimes their hearing is keener than at other times. Ezra, the post-exilic leader who took refuge in a narrow nationalism, did not hear as clearly as the unknown poet of the exile whom we call Second Isaiah, whose vision of the Suffering Servant shaped the ministry of our Lord. Perhaps the mocking skepticism of the Preacher in Ecclesiastes, who declares "All is vanity," is not so sure a response as the passionate cries of some of the psalms, but each represents an authentic effort to answer the question of meaning. A faithful response can be to name the darkness when darkness is the experience.

> My God, my God,
> why hast thou forsaken me?

The first Christians were Jews, and they came out of the rich heritage of Hebrew theology. They knew that the deepest experience the human being can have is the act of trust called faith. "I know," St. Paul is remembered to have said in the first letter to Timothy, "whom I have believed." Faith is its own kind of knowledge. Paul says, "Trust, and then you will know." So as their forebears had looked at the world and said, "In the beginning God..." without any need to develop proof, so the disciples met a young Galilean and called him Lord, and the communities they founded left their testimonies in four remarkable records we know as gospels.

What we have in the Bible is the record of hundreds of years in which the two communities of faith looked at the experiences of their lives and asked what these experiences meant. The communities have left a record of what it meant to them in that collection of books we call the Bible, and that record can only be really understood from within the continuing life of their spiritual heirs. The question we must put to the records they have left behind is not "Which is right?" but questions like "What does it mean?" and "What did it mean for them?" and "What does it mean for us?"

Chapter Two

THE BIBLICAL
STORY

And now the biblical story as I see it. The Bible begins with a great faith statement. "In the beginning God...." That is not the only way to account for the beginning. Others propose a big bang, or a titanic struggle between many gods, but the ancient Hebrews were willing to stake their life on one God, and they went on to an even more daring statement— "God created." Not only is there meaning behind all that there is, but that meaning is for us.

Creation is an act of love, and so the Bible begins with a vulnerable God. To love is to be vulnerable. The story of creation bears that fact out. The lover seeks the beloved. The lover is not complete without the beloved.

James Weldon Johnson, in the second of his poetic recreations of the old black preacher in *God's Trombones*, begins his poem "The Creation" with these words:

And God stepped out on space,
And God said: I'm lonely,
I'll make me a world.

The lonely God—the God who needs that God's creation. It is an amazing thought, but it is borne out by the biblical story.

So the biblical poem goes on. God created a good creation, and then, the old black preacher says,

Then God walked around,
And God looked around
On all that he had made.
He looked at his sun,
And he looked at his moon,
And he looked at his little stars;
He looked on his world
With all its living things,
And God said: I'm lonely still.[1]

You see, God had created a good creation. After every act the poet has the refrain, "And God saw that it was good." That goodness means perfection, in the sense that each star and plant and animal was as God determined it to be.

There was no freedom in creation. There was no choice in creation. Apple trees could only be apple trees. Lions could only be lions. Only human beings could choose to be other than God wanted them to be.

We have missed the meaning of what it is to be created in the image of God. It has nothing to do with looking like God. It has to do with God's freedom.

Paul's understanding of God's words, "Jacob I loved, but Esau I hated" is very troubling to our modern minds. Paul couples it with God's word to Moses, "I will be gracious to whom I will be gracious, and will show mercy on whom I will show mercy." For Karl Barth this verse describes the freedom of God, who is "regal, sovereign, unbounded and incomprehensible," and other commentators pick up on this note of freedom. The issue is one of election, and it makes no sense if God is not free. That freedom is the image stamped on only one creature—the human being. That creature could choose to be as God wanted it to be, or it was free to choose another way.

God's creation could not love. The only creature that can love is the free creature. The only creature that can love is the creature free not to love.

So the biblical poet recounts the risk of God:

> Then God said, "Let us make man in our image."...So God created man in his own image, in the image of God he created him; male and female he created them. (Genesis 1:26–27)

The black preacher says:

> Then God sat down—
> On the side of a hill where he could think;
> By a deep, wide river he sat down;
> With his head in his hands,
> God thought and thought,
> Till he thought: I'll make me a man![2]

But after that final act of creation, the refrain "And God saw that it was good" does not appear. Not for five verses, when the whole creation is reviewed, do we again have the refrain, "And God saw that it was good."

Human beings were not created good, perfect, programmed. Human beings were created *free*. Of all God's creations, human beings alone had the choice of whether to respond to God as God wanted them to, or to go another way. The Lover is always vulnerable to the beloved. The beloved may always say no.

A vulnerable God. What a conception! Gordon Cosby of the Church of the Saviour, an ecumenical community in Washington, D. C., used to say that a cross was in the heart of God before one went up on Calvary. Theodore Wedel of the College of Preachers called the Bible a great love story of God, the Lover, wooing human beings, the beloved, and said it is a story with a happy ending. I have a friend, not so optimistic as Canon Wedel, who says the verdict is not in yet.

The biblical witness is, I believe, that God will never crush our freedom. The God of the biblical story will never participate in the human arrogance of having it our way and claiming it is for the other's good.

And so into God's good creation comes the free creature, who says no to God's dream of "a friendly world of friendly folk beneath a friendly sky," as Howard Thurman, a black mystic, described God's good creation.

The second and third chapters of Genesis give a much older account than the first of the beginning of things and the establishment of the way God and human beings were to live together. They try to answer the question, "Why is life not better than it is?"

The story begins with the completion of the universe and God taking a rest. Then God created *adam* and put him in the garden in Eden where he had a pleasant place to live, plenty to eat, work to do, and only one command to obey—to refrain from eating of the tree of the knowledge of good and evil. Then God decided it was not good for *adam* to be alone, and he decided to give the new creature a fit companion. God created all the animals and birds, and set *adam* to the task of naming them.

That task accomplished without finding any creature suitable for *adam*, God puts him into a deep sleep and takes one of his ribs. From this rib God makes a woman and brings her to the man. She arouses excitement as no other creature has, and the man greets her joyously.

Into all this bliss comes the serpent, "more subtle than any beast of the field," the narrator tells us. He and the woman have quite a conversation. The snake says to Eve,

"Did God say, 'You shall not eat of any tree of the garden'?"

Eve corrects him. "We may eat of any tree except the one in the center, lest we die." But the serpent pooh-poohs the idea. "If you eat of that tree you will become like God, knowing good and evil."

Eve is intrigued. She takes some fruit, eats, finds it good, and gives it to Adam, who also eats. And, the story says, their eyes were opened and they knew they were naked, so they got busy and made coverings for themselves.

God's dream of a friendly world of friendly folk beneath a friendly sky is shattered. God is someone to hide from. Human beings cast accusations at other creatures. There is enmity between human beings and other creatures, between men and women. Work becomes a curse, and the continuation of the race a painful burden. The temptation from the most subtle of the beasts of the field was too much to be refused. "You shall be as gods, knowing absolutely what is good and what is evil." That temptation was too great. God's great dream foundered on the rock of human freedom, and we call that moment the Fall.

I call it the first of many falls, the choice human beings make against the lordship, the sovereignty, of God. The rest of the biblical story is the record of the actions of God to win that free creature back, the Lover seeking the beloved.

Following the stories of universal history—the flood, the ark, the tower of Babel—the book of Genesis settles down to the history of the Hebrew peoples. The next great act in the drama is the calling of the Israelites. Calling, election, chosenness in the biblical story is always calling, chosenness, election for God's purposes. God's purpose is to restore the fallen world, to reconcile the rebellious creature to the Creator. In the twelfth chapter of Genesis we read:

> Now the LORD said to Abram, "Go from your country and your kindred and your father's house to the land that I will show you. And I will make of you a great nation, and I will bless you, and make your name great, so that you will be a blessing...; and by you all the families of the earth shall bless themselves. (Genesis 12:1–3)

The story of Abram, the father of the Hebrew people, begins with an act of faith. Biblical faith is not intellectual assent to a proposition. It is risking that God is worthy of trust.

Here is Abram, a stable member of a stable community. God says, Leave it all and go to a land I will show you. He is not even told where or what the land is. Just go— and Abram goes. The other interesting thing about the call is it is not for Abram alone, for "by you all the families of the earth shall bless themselves." Abram is on a mission. God's purpose to restore the world has begun. The task for which the chosen people were chosen has begun.

The journey is not easy, and Abram is not steadfastly heroic. To save his life he passes his wife Sarai off as his sister, and he has territorial problems with his nephew, Lot, but God keeps reassuring him, gets him out of scrapes, and renews his promise to make him the father of a great nation.

I remember the picture in my childhood Bible of Abram looking up at the night sky and hearing the voice of God, "Number the stars if you can. So shall your descendants be." And then the ancient scribe wrote the line that was to be so meaningful to Paul as he developed his powerful understanding of faith: "And he believed the Lord; and he reckoned it to him as righteousness."

The story moves on through the use and abuse of the Egyptian maid Hagar when Abram and Sarai try to take into their own hands the fulfilling of God's promises—a story that does no honor to either Abram or Sarai—and then on to the climax of the story, the establishment of the covenant, the name change, and the seal of circumcision as the sign of the people of the covenant, the people blessed in order to be a blessing.

Abraham was the first of the patriarchs, and the last was Joseph. Joseph was probably the most annoying teenager the world has ever known, great-grandson of Abram and Sarai, grandson of Isaac, through whom the promise was to be fulfilled, son of Jacob, the "wandering Aramean" of the harvest liturgy. He was a favorite of his father, who spoiled him shamelessly. While his brothers had to do the work necessary to keep the homefires burning, Joseph strolled around in a long-sleeved robe, which is erroneously translated "a coat of many colors"; it was simply an outfit that indicated its wearer was not going to do any work. Not only did he live a life of leisure in the presence of his hardworking brothers, but he was a dreamer who told his dreams to all and sundry, a dreamer whose dreams had him on top and his father and hardworking brothers bowing down to him.

Enough was enough, and his brothers conspired first to kill him and then to sell him into slavery.

I always think one of the greatest transformations in human history happened to Joseph between the time he was tossed in that pit by his brothers and when he was pulled out, sold, and taken to Egypt. His fortunes did not immediately improve in Egypt because he attracted the attention of his master's wife; and when he rebuffed her, she had Joseph tossed in prison.

There, however, he again demonstrated his ability to interpret dreams, and when the Pharaoh began to have disturbing dreams of scrawny ears of corn consuming full ears of corn, and lean cattle devouring fat cattle, Joseph was called in to interpret. His interpretation and his solution so impressed the Pharaoh that he was put in charge of the preparations for the famine and the administration of the nation.

Egypt became the bread basket of the world, and to Egypt came his brothers seeking food. Joseph's dream of their bowing down to him came true. When the brothers bow their faces to the ground before this exalted personage, Joseph recognizes them at once and begins a long cat-and-mouse game with them. He accuses them of being spies and insists the only way they can prove their innocence is by leaving one of them behind as hostage while the other nine return to the father and bring back the youngest son.

Their father Jacob treasures Benjamin as the only child of his beloved Rachel left to him, but he finally gives in. So back they go with the young lad, but Joseph has another trick up his sleeve. He wines and dines them sumptuously, but hides his silver cup in Benjamin's sack and sends his soldiers after them when they depart. The cup is found in Benjamin's belongings, and back they all go to the governor. Joseph, of course, generously pardons them all except for Benjamin, the ostensible thief. Of course, this solution is not tolerable, as Judah explains to Joseph in a private session, and Joseph, dissolved in tears, makes himself known to his brothers. There follows a happy reunion. All the family comes down to Egypt, and that is the story of how the Israelites got into Egypt in the first place.

The book of Exodus, the beginning of the historical account, starts off with the grim news, "There arose a new king in Egypt, who did not know Joseph." By that time the Israelites had greatly multiplied and were perceived as a threat to the native population. All efforts at population control failing, the Egyptians resorted to genocide, killing the male children.

One resourceful young Hebrew mother planned a way for her son to escape by putting him in a basket and placing the basket by the river bank among the reeds so that the daughter of Pharaoh could see it when she came to the river with her maidens to bathe. The princess is attracted by the child's cries and takes pity on him, recognizing that he is an ill-fated Hebrew infant. Moses' sister, obviously instructed by Moses' mother, immediately offers to find the princess a Hebrew nursemaid, and Moses' mother is promptly on the scene. The princess hires her to nurse the baby; and when the child is weaned, she brings him to the princess, having fed him, you may be sure, all the stories of Abraham and Isaac and Jacob and Joseph along with his mother's milk.

Moses grew up in Pharaoh's household as an Egyptian prince with a Hebrew memory. His championship of the Hebrews made it necessary for him to flee Egypt, but the flight did not take him beyond the reach of God.

> Go down, Moses,
> Way down in Egypt land,
> Tell old Pharaoh
> To let my people go.

Finally after many plagues and much hardening of heart, Pharaoh did let the children of Israel go.

The night of their departure was an awesome night and is memorialized in both the Hebrew and Christian liturgies. The Lord gave Moses instructions as to how they were to prepare for that night. Each household was to kill an unblemished lamb and sprinkle some of the blood on the lintel of the houses and on the doorposts. They were to eat it roasted with unleavened bread. Nothing was to be left over, and they were to eat in haste, loins girded, shoes on feet, staff in hand. It was the Lord's Passover. The angel of death swept through the land, sparing those houses where the blood of a lamb was sprinkled on the lintel of the door, and the Hebrew children marched out to freedom.

Forty years in the wilderness lay ahead of them. Forty years was the length of time it took for the generation born in slavery to die out and a new generation, born and bred in the wilderness—symbolized by Joshua, who had been Moses' chief lieutenant—to come of age and take control. Forty years was also time enough for God to establish a covenant relationship with this chosen people, give them a form of government and a way of life that would be a light to the Gentiles, and show all the world what life under the lordship of God was like.

From Exodus 19 through the books of Leviticus, Numbers, and Deuteronomy, that way of life is proclaimed. It begins with God's direction to Moses in the wilderness of Sinai:

> Thus you shall say to the house of Jacob, and tell the people of Israel: You have seen what I did to the Egyptians, and how I bore you on eagles' wings and brought you to myself. Now therefore, if you will obey my voice and keep my covenant, you shall be my own possession among all peoples; for all the earth is mine, and you shall be to me a kingdom of priests and a holy nation. These are the words which you shall speak to the children of Israel. (Exodus 19:3b–6)

Moses dutifully delivered the message, and the people responded, "All that the LORD has spoken we will do." The covenant was set.

The minutiae of detail in succeeding books have obscured for many Christians the majesty of the law and made them draw a false dichotomy between law and grace. For the children of Israel, the law *was* grace, a gift by which their creator and deliverer bound them and the holy God into something new in the world and something new for the world. Walter Brueggemann calls this new thing the alternative community of Moses:

> The reality emerging out of the Exodus is not just a new religion or a new religious idea or a vision of freedom but the emergence of a new social community in history, a community that has an historical body, that had to devise laws, patterns of governance and order, norms of right and wrong, and sanctions of accountability. The participants in the Exodus found themselves, undoubtedly surprising to them, involved in the intentional formation of a new social community to match the vision of God's freedom.[3]

The Hebrew people were called to another way of life than that of the nations around them, but instead they chose the way of the kingdoms of the world. They chose kings.

The first king was Saul, tall and handsome, but he had many problems—not the least of which was David, waiting in the wings. Saul was a tragic figure, more like the judges of the rough days of establishing the nation than like the imperial monarch of the Solomonic empire. When we first meet him, he is looking for his father's asses. He is considerate of his servant, respectful before the holy man, reticent about his anointing, and generous to his enemies.

In *Understanding the Old Testament*, Bernhard Anderson is very sympathetic to Saul and sees him as a heroic figure who lived in a transitional period between the collapse of an old order—the tribal confederacy of the period of the judges—and the birth of a new order, the nation state of David. Saul could not find a home in either place. He was rejected by Samuel, stern representative of the old order, and threatened by David, vigorous herald of the new. In song and story they sing of David:

David was a shepherd boy
He killed Goliath and shouted for joy.
Little David, play on your harp,
Hallelu!

King David was truly a figure of heroic attributes—poet, musician, soldier, lover, administrator, believer. He fixed on the hearts and minds of the Hebrew people for all time what a king should be like, and ever afterward they looked for "great David's greater son." But the seeds for the destruction of a nation are sown in one age and reaped in another. David died in his bed, and so did Solomon, his son, the ostentatious imperial monarch, the first man to rule over Israel not because God chose him, but because his father was king. There is no record of God's prophet anointing Solomon; instead, he was the beneficiary of court intrigues.

The blow fell on Solomon's son Rehoboam.

By that time the people realized they had made a mistake in choosing to have kings, and they wanted to return to the covenant life of the wilderness. Unrest stirred in the land. Solomon had put a man named Jeroboam, whom he had spotted as industrious, in charge of his gangs of forced laborers. This same Jeroboam, who must have chafed at Solomon's violation of the way the people of God were to treat one another under the covenant, and made his objections known, was met one day by the prophet Ahijah. In a characteristic prophetic act, Ahijah tore into twelve pieces the garment he was wearing and gave ten pieces to Jeroboam, declaring God's intention of taking the kingdom away from Solomon because he "has not walked in my ways, doing what is right in my sight and keeping my statutes and my ordinances" (1 Kings 11:33).

Solomon got wind of the intended rebellion and Jeroboam fled to Egypt, where he stayed until Solomon's death. He came then and presented to Rehoboam his petition for change. After conferring with his counselors, Rehoboam returned a smart answer: "My father chastised you with whips, but I will chastise you with scorpions," and the people answered the king,

> What portion have we in David?
> We have no inheritance in the son of Jesse.
> To your tents, O Israel! (1 Kings 12:16)

Scholars say the subsequent revolt was prompted by theological as well as economic concerns. The northern tribes wanted some limitation of the king's power in their region, in accordance with their theology of the Mosaic covenant. Even though Jeroboam received a bad press from the Deuteronomic historian of this period, his intention was really to renew Israel's devotion to the God of the covenant and provide a strong religious foundation for his kingdom. You can't go home again, however, and the rebellion against Rehoboam only resulted in the kingdom's being split in two, the northern kingdom of Israel and the southern kingdom of Judah.

The time of troubles was upon the people of God. Beset by strong enemy nations, first the richer northern kingdom fell to a ruthless conqueror, Assyria, and then the southern kingdom to Babylon. They had missed their high calling to be a new thing in the world and show all people another possibility for life.

Defeat and exile awaited the chosen people, but the dream of God did not die. God had offered to the whole human race the possibility of life under the sovereignty of God, life in covenant relationship with the Creator. It had been refused. Then the possibility was offered to one people, but they too missed the mark.

Then God offered the possibility to a *remnant* of that people—disciplined by war, humiliated by exile. Would that remnant understand? The possibility was there—the possibility is always present. A poet of the exile whom we call Second Isaiah caught this possibility in the vision of the Suffering Servant (Isaiah 41:8–42; 49:1–6; 50:4–9; 52:13–53:12). Because the early Christians identified the Servant with Jesus—and I think Jesus himself pondered the Servant message as a model for his ministry—we have missed the greatness of the poet.

Scholars have wrestled with the question of whether the Servant is an individual or the nation of Israel, but the most important aspect of these poems is the fact that they are a startling new response. Not by power—not by kingly dynasties or military might—but by the spirit of the Lord, the God who acts in ways that are not the ways of human beings. The Lord is doing a new thing. Who will understand it?

But Ezra saw another way. Ezra was a scribe after the exile who saw close adherence to the law as the best way to uphold the covenant. Second Isaiah was the visionary, Ezra the pragmatist. The people asked for specifics: What would it look like to be God's servant? What would we be doing? Ezra found the answer in the minutiae of the law, and the religion of the scribes was born.

The biblical story is one of a free God who created free creatures to be in fellowship with their Creator. The free creatures could not trust the divine way, and God, respecting their freedom, set in motion a plan to win them back. The plan began with the calling of a chosen people to show the world a way to live marked by the love and compassion and justice and mercy of God. God entered into a covenant relationship with this people and brought them to a place of honor and eminence in the world. They were attracted, however, by the opulence and rituals of the rest of the world and turned from the ways that had shaped them. Despite the voices of their prophets, they missed the mark of their high calling.

How would God call this people back?

The biblical story is that God then entered history to show the world in Jesus the Christ the glory and the promise—the cost and the reward—of life lived in absolute allegiance to a way that is not the world's way.

Jesus was born in Bethlehem of Judea in the days of Herod the king, when Caesar Augustus was emperor of Rome. You cannot get much more historical than that: a specific place, a specific time, and a specific person. (No springing full-grown from the head of Zeus, like the gods of classical mythology.) For thirty years he lived a largely unremarkable life in a small rural setting. He took care of his mother, who might have been widowed—Joseph drops out of the story when Jesus is twelve, and his need to care for his mother may account for the late start of his ministry. He took part in village life, noting everything— children, flowers, laborers, animals—that would be the content of his teaching. Then, at about the age of thirty, he embarked on his mission, preaching the kingdom of God.

Jesus had a significant religious experience in which he understood who he was and what he was called to be. That baptism was followed by a lengthy period in which he wrestled through how best to present to his people God's ancient call to them to be something new in the world. By concern for the marginalized? That had always been a significant part of Israel's covenant with God, but it could be distorted into a means of getting credit with God instead of an expression of the very nature of God. By taking over the kingdoms of the world and compelling them to serve God? But God's ends can only be achieved by God's means. By a spectacular demonstration of the good effects of allegiance to God? But to demand proof from God denies God's omnipotence. The only right relationship between God and God's people is gratitude for what God has done and faith in what God will do.

That is life in the kingdom of God.

Jesus set out to live it. He gathered a band of followers, imbued them with his vision, and lived out with them life in the kingdom of God. That way brought him into conflict with the kingdoms of the world.

The record is that Jesus was amazingly ordinary. Flesh and blood will not reveal to you who I am, he is remembered as having said. Only by the power of the Holy Spirit can you know who I am. By the grace of God something in you will respond to something in me, and you will know. Each gospel is an answer to Jesus' great question, "Who do you say that I am?"

In Mark's gospel, Jesus is the incarnation of the reign of God. He comes onto the scene of history, announcing the kingdom of God is at hand. He is a young man in a hurry; the word "immediately" is used more often in Mark than anywhere else in the whole Bible. Where Jesus appears life is changed, restored to the good creation. More miracles occur in this gospel than in any other.

According to Matthew, Jesus is the fulfillment of the law, the consummate rabbi. Matthew divides his gospel into five great teaching sections to correspond to the first five books of the Bible—the new Torah. The constant theme is, "You have heard it said of old, but I say unto you. . . ." God's law is fulfilled not just by refraining from negative acts, but by living out new relationships with other human beings.

For Luke, Jesus is the friend of sinners, the poor, the outcasts. Whereas wise men came to the cradle in Matthew's version, Luke's has lowly shepherds, and in Jesus' inaugural sermon, he reminds Israel of her ancient mission "to preach good news to the poor... to proclaim release to the captives and recovering of sight to the blind, to set at liberty those who are oppressed, to proclaim the acceptable year of the Lord" (Luke 4:18–19). And he tells the attentive audience, "Today this scripture has been fulfilled in your hearing."

Finally, for John, Jesus is the Word made flesh. With seven great signs and in seven great "I am" statements, Jesus proclaims who he is. The feeding of the multitude is reported by all the evangelists, but in the Fourth Gospel, the meaning is clearly given: Jesus says, "I am the bread of life." Lazarus is raised from the dead after Jesus assures his sister, "I am the resurrection and the life."

Each gospel is a record of how our community experienced Jesus of Nazareth. Each one states, "This is what we believe God was saying to us in this man." And here the biblical story ends, with the early church trying to make sense of the Word made flesh. The biblical story is ended, but the revelation goes on. How do *we* make sense of it?

How we answer that question, I think, will be significant for our understanding of what the church is. Is it a part of God's continuing work to create a people who will be God's instrument to restore a fallen world to the dream of a good creation of love and peace and justice? Or is the church a mentor for chosen individuals, guiding them through this world with the best it has to offer and preparing them for the best of the world to come?

1. James Weldon Johnson, *God's Trombones* (New York: Viking, 1927), 19.
2. Johnson, *Trombones*, 19–20.
3. Walter Brueggemann, *The Prophetic Imagination* (Philadelphia: Fortress, 1978), 16–17.

Chapter Three

THE REJECTION
OF THE DREAM

When I was a little child in the Baptist Church, we used to sing a hymn that matches a painting by William Holman. A copy of the painting hung in the sanctuary of the church. It is called *The Light of the World* and has a tender story behind it. When Hunt found out his painting was going to hang in an exclusive chapel in Oxford, he painted a copy of his own picture for St. Paul's in London so that everybody could see it. The painting shows the risen Christ bearing all the marks of his crucifixion, knocking at a fast closed door. The hymn goes:

O Jesus, thou art standing
Outside the fast closed door
In lowly patience waiting
To pass the threshold o'er.

We bear the name of Christians
His name and sign we bear,

Oh, shame, thrice shame upon us,
To keep Him standing there.

I think of that simple, unsophisticated bit of religious
verse when I contemplate what I call the three falls, the
three rejections by human beings of the dream of God.

In the Genesis story God created a good world and
created human beings to be the crown of that creation,
in the image of God, and to be God's representative in
that creation. Psalm 8 celebrates this creation:

O Lord our Governor,
    how exalted is your Name in all the world!
Out of the mouths of infants and children
    your majesty is praised above the heavens.
You have set up a stronghold against your adversaries,
    to quell the enemy and the avenger.
When I consider your heavens, the work
    of your fingers,
    the moon and the stars you have set in their courses,
What is man that you should be mindful of him?
    the son of man that you should seek him out?
You have made him but little lower than the angels;
    you adorn him with glory and honor;
You give him mastery over the works of your hands;
    you put all things under his feet;
All sheep and oxen,
    even the wild beasts of the field,
The birds of the air, the fish of the sea,
    and whatsoever walks in the paths of the sea.
O Lord our Governor,
    how exalted is your Name in all the world!

Walter Brueggemann, a teacher and scholar of the Old
Testament, calls this psalm an advance for the articula-
tion of creation faith.[1] Not only is creation well ordered,

but the human person is acknowledged to be God's regent in the governance of creation.

With the phrase "you give him mastery," the psalmist picks up the idea of the poet of the first chapter of Genesis. God tells the human creatures to have dominion over all other living things, but the word "dominion" has given our age—with its concern for the ruthless despoiling of earth and seas, plants and animals—occasion to rethink our understanding of this directive. Did the ancient poet really see God as giving human beings a directive to pillage and destroy as we have done?

Brueggemann instead prefers the term "regent," one who rules on behalf of someone else and according to the wishes of someone else. Another scholar recalls that powerful earthly kings of the time, in order to enforce their claim to dominion, erected images of themselves in the provinces of their empires where they did not appear in person. Similarly, human beings are placed upon earth as God's sovereign emblem. Because of the human dominion, the whole created order receives the dignity belonging to this special domain of God's sovereignty. Responsible action, rather than ruthless exploitation, is called for by these biblical poets.

The fact of human regency, however, is framed in verses 1 and 9 by what Brueggemann calls "an envelope of praise to the regal Creator." The psalm begins and ends with, "O Lord our Governor, how exalted is your Name in all the world!" Human beings are most fully human when they realize that they are creatures and give joyful response to the Creator. All that we are and all that we have comes from God. We are a part of God's dream of a good creation, and we are to use our freedom to do God's will. That is the biblical understanding of creation.

Compare it to Shakespeare's psalm-like praise of humanity.

What a piece of work is a man!
   how noble in reason! how infinite in faculty!
in form and moving how express and admirable!
in action how like an angel!
in apprehension how like a god!
   the beauty of the world! the paragon of animals!

Gone is the biblical picture of a Creator God. Renaissance man does not need that hypothesis, for the Renaissance is concerned with humanity. The subject matter of Michelangelo's masterpieces was taken from the Bible but, as Will Durant observed, "The theme and object of his art was the human body." Several centuries later, Swinburne captured the Renaissance spirit in the "Hymn of Man":

Glory to Man in the highest!
For Man is the master of things.

Truth to tell, even biblical man found God burdensome. Listen to Job, the protagonist of the great drama whose unknown author questioned the ways of God:

What is man, that thou dost make so much of him,
   and that thou dost set thy mind upon him,
dost visit him every morning,
   and test him every moment? (Job 7:17–18)

And my favorite psalm, rightly read, I think also expresses the burden of an all-encompassing God:

Where can I go then from your Spirit?
   where can I flee from your presence?
If I climb up to heaven, you are there;
   if I make the grave my bed, you are there also.
                    (Psalm 139:6–7)

At that moment the psalmist was expressing no pleasure. God, an ever-present God, was experienced as a burden.

The three falls are those three moments when human beings broke their covenant with such a God. The first fall, the Genesis story, is a masterpiece. Adam and Eve are living happily with each other and with God. Kierkegaard calls it the state of dreaming innocence. The gloomy Dane of philosophy thinks the fall was a good thing; he called it the fall upward. How else could we have become human? he asks.

The serpent sidles up to the woman, considering her, I think, the livelier of the two. "Hath God said," he asks subtly, in the King James Version, "Ye shall not eat of every tree of the garden?"

The woman sets the record straight: "We may eat of the fruit of the trees of the garden," she corrects him, "but God has told us that if we eat from the tree in the middle of the garden, we will die."

"Oh no," the serpent laughs, "you won't die. God knows that then you will have as much knowledge as he has. You will be like God, knowing good and evil."

When the woman heard that, she was a goner. She not only ate—she shared it with her husband. Kenyan women with whom I worked one summer thought Eve was pretty generous and outgoing.

But then there was the awesome moment of reckoning with God. The great question: "Where are you?" For upon eating the fruit, as the Bible has it, their eyes were opened and they knew that they were naked, so they got busy and sewed fig leaves together and made aprons for themselves. Then they heard the sound of the Lord God walking in the garden in the cool of the day, and they hid. The Lord God called to the man, "Where are you?" It is the first question God addresses to human beings in the biblical story.

When I taught school, we used to joke about our students who were asleep behind their most attentive stares. "Where are you?" Just because you are sitting in a lecture hall does not mean you are with the lecturer. Or have you ever been in a discussion group in which one participant comes up with an observation that you think is from outer space? That is probably where the person has been.

"Where are you?" God asks Adam and Eve. Not in that good creation that God dreamed.

Adam replies, "I heard your voice in the garden, and I was afraid, because I was naked, and I hid myself." Eden is spoiled. Fear and hiddenness have entered the good creation.

"Who told you that you were naked?" God asked. "Have you eaten of the tree of which I commanded you not to eat?"

And then Adam's shattering response. "The woman whom you gave to be with me, she gave me of the tree, and I did eat." The epitome of what sin is all about.

"The woman *you* gave me," answered Adam. In other words, God is responsible.

She gave me of the tree. The other one, *she* is responsible.

And I did eat. But I have no responsibility for what I ate. I had no freedom not to eat.

The epitome of sin is separation from God, from the companion, from myself. No God, no community, no freedom. The crown of God's creation is fallen, and the Bible has many images for this state:

...his hand will be against every man and every man's hand against him.... (Genesis 16:12)

I will make your heavens like iron and your earth like brass. (Leviticus 26:19)

For I do not do the good I want, but the evil I do not want is what I do. (Romans 7:19)

When we waste our time talking about sin as individual acts—usually individual acts someone else is doing—we miss the power of the biblical idea of sin. Jesus was very incisive in his judgment on this response to individual acts: paying attention to the splinter in someone else's eye while ignoring the log in our own. Sin is a misuse of human freedom that separates us from God, from other people, even from ourselves. In fact our very concern about other people's sins is a manifestation of sin. Sin is separation. The wholeness of creation is broken.

In time and in eternity, God's dream of a friendly world of friendly folk beneath a friendly sky was rejected. "Eternity" does not mean time without end; it means that dimension in which time does not figure.

The first fall was in eternity. It is the myth that describes for our tradition the existential nature of the human condition. Adam and Eve have neither race nor nationality. We are all Adam and Eve, and we repeat that proud rejection of God's way, hour by hour, generation by generation. The saying "In Adam's fall / We sinned all" came out of destructive theology, a theology that focused more on the individual sins of men and women than on the redemptive love of God, but it points to an existential truth. St. Paul puts it more ambiguously: as in Adam all died, so in Christ shall all be made alive.

The very essence of God's gift is community—a people called out to witness to the dream of God. The rejection of community is individualism, deified in the American ethos as "rugged individualism." That was why the hardest thing for young white people of goodwill during the 1960s to accept was the charge of the blacks that they bore the stain of slavery. "I never owned a slave," they declared. "You stand here, profiting from that legacy," the blacks returned. The charge was not understood in the sixties. It is not understood today. Instead we say, "I made it—why can't you?"

The double irony—and the proof that Adam and Eve, the ones who fell, have neither race nor nationality—is that some blacks do not understand it either. They still buy into the destructive American dream that anyone who tries hard enough can make it. It's all up to the individual. God's gift of community, with all its cost and all its promise, is rejected.

Even now it is still hard for people of goodwill to accept our corporate guilt for Hiroshima. Sojourners, a pacifist community in Washington, D. C., holds a penitential service every August 6, but they are never overwhelmed by crowds. "It saved American lives," I recently heard a woman say, reminding me of the caustic prayer, "Dear God, bless me and my wife, my son John and his wife, us four and no more."

You have to draw the line somewhere, we protest. We can't save everybody. So the question comes down to, whom do we save? Folks who look like us? Think like us? Handle the dinner flatware—pardon me, silver—like us?

Kin altruism?

Who gets into your air raid shelter?

But you can't make a god out of community either, I hear someone protest. Very true, but why make a god out of anything? Isn't the Lord God enough?

Aye, there's the rub. The Lord God is an ambiguous symbol. It points to a reality that I, I as a human being, cannot fully comprehend. "As the heavens are higher than the earth," God says, "so are my ways higher than your ways and my thoughts than your thoughts." But we cannot bear ambiguity. We have to know absolutely what is good and what is evil.

The meaning of ambiguity is going in two directions at the same time, which is very distressing for those of us who want to know, "Which is right?" Nothing is more distressing to us than people who see both sides of the issue. One of the distressing things about them is they

46

never get anything done. They spend all their time weighing the pros and cons so that when they do act, they can be sure they are right. That's why polls are so popular. If the majority of people are thinking it, or are doing it, then "it" must be right. History bears witness to the fact that the majority is not necessarily right. It's just loud, or powerful.

Why do we have this need to be right? It gives us power. We have a mandate to stamp out what's wrong. It gives us comfort. We have an assured place among the righteous. It gives us certainty. We do not have to worry about doubt anymore.

The Christian church succumbs to the temptation to know absolutely when it calls doubt the opposite of faith. Doubt is not the opposite of faith. Fear is. Fear will not risk that even if I am wrong, I will trust that if I move today by the light that is given me, knowing it is only finite and partial, I will know more and different things tomorrow than I know today, and I can be open to the new possibility I cannot even imagine today.

In the first fall, I usurped the place of God. There is no God. There is only I. There is no Other. There is only I. We became lonely, separated, fearful human beings. Not the good world God created.

The next act in the drama of redemption was the calling of a particular people, Israel, which set the stage for the second fall. They were called to live in a covenant relationship with God that the world might see the kind of life God intended for all creation. This covenant began with God reminding the Israelites of God's power and God's dream. The Israelites had been delivered from their Egyptian masters, they had come through the wilderness to Mount Sinai, and now they were to hear what their new life was to be like.

> You have seen what I did to the Egyptians, and how I bore you on eagles' wings and brought you to myself. Now, therefore, if you will obey my voice and keep my covenant, you shall be my own possession among all peoples; for all the earth is mine, and you shall be to me a kingdom of priests and a holy nation. (Exodus 19:4–6)

That statement is the preamble for the commandments that were to guide the life of this special people, this nation chosen to work God's will in the world, chosen to show the world another way to live. The laws by which they were to live governed every facet of their lives, not to be a burden, but so that every facet of their lives would witness to another possibility for human life.

Every seventh year the land is to lie fallow that the poor may eat. Every fiftieth year—the year of Jubilee—everything is to be returned to its original state, all debts cancelled, all relationships restored. The land cannot be sold in perpetuity, for the land is God's. They are not to oppress the stranger, for they are to remember they were strangers in the land of Egypt. The widows and orphans are to be protected. No interest is to be taken. Not only their religious life, but their economic life, their political life, their legal life, and their social life was to witness to a new possibility.

How was the little band of former slaves to work this out?

It is difficult to know what life in the wilderness was like for the children of Israel. It is hard to glean it from the biblical record written by people who were already frightened by the choice for the kingdoms of the world. We can catch glimpses of it from such tidbits as the year of Jubilee, the prophet Nathan's encounter with King

David, and the energy of the prophets in storming against what the covenant people had become.

In the twenty-fifth chapter of Leviticus there is an extraordinary statement that establishes the Jubilee year:

> And you shall hallow the fiftieth year, and proclaim liberty throughout the land to all its inhabitants; it shall be a jubilee for you, when each of you shall return to his property, and each of you shall return to his family. (Leviticus 25:10)

Reversal is the order of the day, says Robert McAfee Brown.

There was realistic wisdom in ancient Israel. All their multitudinous laws were for the purpose of setting up a system of the equality of everyone before God. There were many checks and balances, provisions for Sabbath rests every seven years, rests for man, woman, beasts, for the land; but they realized that even with the best of intentions, things could go awry, and some could accumulate more power, more goods, more status than others, so every fifty years they planned to start over again.

I do not think it matters whether the Jubilee year ever took place. The vision took into account that the crown of creation was fallen, and justice was not automatic.

Justice was the great concern of the prophets. No concept was more fundamental to the alternative community of Moses and to the Old Testament, or is more ignored by the contemporary devout. In the Old Testament, justice meant righteousness.

We wax dewy-eyed over love in the New Testament, but we ignore justice in the Old so we don't know what we are talking about when we talk about love. Love is justice in action. Love God and your neighbor as yourself. The commandment is one. "How can you love God whom you have not seen," a New Testament writer asks, "if you do not love your neighbor whom you have seen?"

A remarkable witness to this passion for justice in the Hebrew scriptures is the confrontation between the prophet Nathan and King David in the second book of Samuel. David, walking one afternoon on the roof of his palace, spied the beautiful Bathsheba, the wife of one of his officers, performing her ritual monthly ablutions. He had her brought to him, and they slept together. Later she sent David word that she was pregnant. David immediately called Uriah home from the battlefield, favored him with attention and presents from the king, and dispatched him to his house and to Bathsheba. Uriah, however, did not go home. On learning of this disconcerting fact, David demanded to know why Uriah had not gone home. Uriah earnestly protested he could not go to his wife while his comrades with the holy symbol of the ark were enduring the privations of the battlefield. David tried again, this time plying Uriah with food and drink at the king's table, but even while drunk, Uriah held to his soldier's duty.

In desperation, David sent him back to the field with a note to the commanding general that Uriah was to be placed in the battle where he would be sure to be killed. And it was done.

But David did not reckon with the passionate morality of a wild prophet. Nathan charged into David's palace and confronted him. He told him a parable of two men in the city, one rich, one poor. He movingly recounted the contrast between the two, the rich man having many flocks and herds; the poor man having only a lamb that was like one of the family. When the rich man had a guest, however, instead of taking one of his many sheep, he took the poor man's lamb, killed it, and served it to his guest. What, he asked, did the king think of such a man?

David fell into the trap and swore that the man who did such a terrible thing deserved to die. "You are the man," Nathan declared (2 Samuel 12:7).

It was a remarkable system that allowed such access to the king. Can you imagine getting into the Oval Office?

David heard and heeded the prophet. He was still close enough to the wilderness religion, the alternative community of Moses, to accept the judgment of God on his life. The king was the shaper of the life of the people. Nathan was confronting a system. Justice was a community concern rather than merely an individual concern.

The book of Joshua and the book of Judges give us a further glimpse into the struggle of the wilderness and conquest period. Joshua is a more romanticized version and suggests the Israelites made a lightning conquest of the promised land, but the harsh book of Judges gives a more realistic picture. Most scholars agree that the actual events of Israel's early history are different from the facts suggested by the narrative. The Canaanites were not systematically annihilated, nor were they completely driven from the land. In fact they made up, to a large extent, the people of the new nation of Israel.

The biblical story is always to be prefaced by, "This is how the faith community that produced the record saw it." It is never to be absolutized as, "This is the way it was." The story always points the way to an understanding of God that is greater than the facts themselves. I think any understanding of the biblical story that fails to see it as a human response only pointing to the dream of God is itself an idolatry.

Bernard Anderson, in his classic work *Understanding the Old Testament*, says:

> The Israelite offensive was continued by means of war, treaty, and the gradual absorption of Canaanites into the Israelite alliance. But at a deeper level an even more important conflict was being fought on the soil of Canaan, a conflict of religious loyalties. In modern language, an ideological struggle was being waged, not just

> a military one.... In the long course of the centuries,
> many victorious nations have been moulded by the
> superior cultures that they vanquished....
> Archaeological excavation in Palestine has shown that
> Israelite life was crude in comparison to the highly
> sophisticated, aristocratic culture of Canaan. Would the
> victor again be overcome by the vanquished?[2]

That strikes me as doubly ironic in view of what I understand as Israel's call. Factual, but ironic.

Israel's call was to witness to a new possibility for humankind, to be something new in the world. It is a sorry story that the people of God long for "the flesh pots of Egypt," the lures of a consumer society with all its glitter and gloss. Over and over the people of God succumb to the temptation to be just like the people around them.

The most striking characteristic of Israel's tribal confederacy was its government by the judges, who were military leaders and internal administrators. The authority of the judge extended beyond the locale of the tribe and was recognized in all the territories of the confederacy.

The history of these charismatic leaders—Gideon, Samson, Deborah—is marked by a continuing pattern. The people of God turn away from God and follow other deities, are defeated by their enemies, and cry out to Yahweh to deliver them. Yahweh raises up a judge to deliver them and they enjoy a subsequent period of peace and prosperity under the judge. Then the cycle repeats itself.

The story of Gideon, one of the longest in the book of Judges, is typical. It begins with an account of apostasy:

> The people of Israel did what was evil in the sight of the LORD; and the LORD gave them into the hand of Midian seven years.... And Israel was brought very low because of Midian, and the people of Israel cried for help to the LORD. (Judges 6:1, 6)

The Midianites were systematically destroying the pro-
duce of Israel's farms, and we first see Gideon as he is in
the act of hiding his food supply. An angel comes and
tells him he has been chosen to free the Israelites from
the Midianites. Gideon is skeptical, but on being con-
vinced, he destroys the altar of the foreign god. This
courageous act inflames him with holy zeal, and he is
ready to do battle for the Lord, although not before he
puts the Lord to the test. The dew has to fall on the
fleece and not on the ground on which it lies. Then it has
to fall on the ground and not on the fleece. God obliges,
and Gideon is ready to do battle. The Lord primes his
army; and with trumpets and torches, Gideon routs the
Midianites and "the land had rest for forty years."

However, there were early indications that the people
of God were not entirely happy with God and God was
not entirely happy with them. The record even says that
when the Israelites were beset by hostile surrounding
tribes, God rejected their pleas for help, reminding them
of past apostasies. The people of God were attracted not
only to the worship of the surrounding nations, but also
to their political organization—there was an uncertain
quality about the succession of judges compared to the
stable dynasties of kings. The Israelites had even
approached Gideon and asked him and his descendants
to rule over them, but he refused in no uncertain terms:
"I will not rule over you, and my son will not rule over
you; the LORD will rule over you" (Judges 8:23).

By the time of the last of the judges, Samuel, the
tribes were more secure in the new land, and they had
space and time to look around and see how their neighbors were doing. Times were changing. The Israelites
noticed that their neighbors had kings, in all their splen-
dor and glory, not pitiful little rough and ready judges
who rose up at a moment's notice to do the job that was

required and passed off the scene with no heirs to carry on their glory.

Samuel was aware of this hankering after the flesh pots of Egypt—there are always the flesh pots of Egypt!—and he tried to ward off the radical change in Israel's government by appointing his sons as judges. But alas, the record reads:

> Yet his sons did not walk in his ways, but turned aside after gain; they took bribes and perverted justice. Then all the elders of Israel gathered together and came to Samuel at Ramah, and said to him, "Behold, you are old and your sons do not walk in your ways; now appoint for us a king to govern us like all the nations." (1 Samuel 8:3–5)

Like all the nations. "We do not want to be different."

Samuel is angry, and surely not a little embarrassed that he must make such a request to God. However, the God of the biblical revelation, with whose patience we become impatient, calmly replies:

> Hearken to the voice of the people in all that they say to you; for they have not rejected you, but they have rejected me from being king over them. (1 Samuel 8:7)

I call that the second great fall in human history, the second time the dream of God founders on the choice of the creatures against the Creator.

In the Garden of Eden God offered the human creatures a way of life in which God would be God and human beings would be the crown of creation, but human beings said no, we want to be God, too.

The first fall.

On the second try, God offered the chosen people a way of life that would testify to a new possibility for human life, absolute trust in God, but the chosen people said, no, we want to be like all the nations. We do not want to live in the uncertainty of the risk that God will raise up leaders when we need them. We want the security of systems and dynasties and human order.

The second fall.

The effect of the second fall, the choice of the kingdoms of this world rather than the kingdom of God, was the setting up of competing gods. I think it is a mistake to say the ancient Hebrews were monotheistic. They knew there were many gods. Their call was to *worship* one god. They were called to make a choice.

"And if you be unwilling to serve the Lord," Joshua told the people,

> Choose this day whom you will serve, whether the gods your fathers served in the region beyond the River, or the gods of the Amorites in whose land you dwell; but as for me and my house, we will serve the LORD. (Joshua 24:15)

In the kingdom of God the citizens are called to make a choice. In the kingdoms of the world, the citizens are pulled this way and that by competing loyalties. There is no center.

I have always considered the third fall, the third time the people of God chose the kingdoms of this world instead of the kingdom of God, to be in the fourth century, when, in the words of an optimistic Christian historian, "the Church subdued the State." I have always thought exactly the opposite—it was the state that subdued the church. The effect of the third fall was to make accommodation the mode of the people of God.

By moving so quickly to post-biblical times for my third fall, I do not mean to exonerate the people of the New Testament from missing the mark of their high calling. I believe the drive toward institutionalization apparent in the closing books of the New Testament, with their concurrent demand for orthodoxy, was a falling away from the awesome freedom offered by God in Jesus the Christ, but that will be the focus of the next chapter.

It is hard for us to understand what happened to the people of God under Constantine. Surely the church got a breathing space from persecution. "Swords that had been drawn to punish were now raised to honor," Roland Bainton wrote.[3] The theologian Charles Williams, in his poetic history of the church, *Descent of the Dove*, remembers that Constantine

> appeared as a messenger from God, covered with gold and precious stones—a magnificent figure, tall and slender, and full of grace and majesty. He blushed; he kept his eyes on the ground; the bishops gestured toward him; he sat down on a throne of gold; he spoke.[4]

The church includes Constantine in its hierarchy of the venerated and proudly points to him as the first Christian emperor—but who had the most to gain from Constantine's "conversion"? Even Dorothy Sayers, most orthodox daughter of the church, has Constantine say in her historically very accurate drama *The Emperor Constantine*: "The Empire needs pulling together—a new focus of faith and energy."[5] Christianity was a potent force, so Constantine, superb strategist that he was, used that force.

Some Christian authors have sought to show that the emperor's conversion was the goal toward which the history of the church and the empire had always been moving, while others have claimed that Constantine was simply a shrewd politician who became aware of the advantages that could be drawn from a conversion. Both positions may be exaggerations, but Constantine's conversion was of a special kind. Normally new converts were put through a long process of instruction and discipline, called the catechumenate, under the guidance of a bishop, yet Constantine never placed himself under the direction of Christian teachers. Not only did he reserve the right to determine his own religious practices, he even intervened in the life of the church, for he considered himself "bishop of bishops." Constantine even put off being baptized until he was dying, because baptism had to be preceded by a long period of instruction and discipline under the guidance of a bishop. The "bishop of bishops" would not submit.

For him the Christian God was a very powerful being who would support him as long as he favored the faithful. When Constantine had churches built and enacted laws favoring Christianity, what he sought was not the good will of Christians, but rather the good will of their God.

Constantine dreamed of restoring the ancient glory of the empire, and he believed that could best be achieved through Christianity. Constantine himself was not changed; the church was. It became the imperial church. Christian worship began to be influenced by imperial protocol. Incense, the sign of respect for the emperor, began to appear in Christian churches. Ministers began dressing in more luxurious garments, processions and choirs developed, and eventually the congregation came to have a less active role in worship.

More important than any of this, however, was the kind of theology that developed. The gospel of good news to the poor now saw riches and pomp as signs of divine favor. The coming kingdom of God was no longer a fundamental theme. In the view of Eusebius, the father of church history, the plan of God had been fulfilled in Constantine and his successors. Beyond the present political order, all that Christians can hope for is their own personal transference into the heavenly kingdom.

As William Langland's epic poem *Piers Plowman* has it:

> When the kindness of Constantine
> gave Holy Church endowments,
> in lands and leases, lordships and servants,
> The Romans heard an angel cry
> on high above them,
> "This day *dos ecclesiae* has drunk venom
> And all who have Peter's power
> are poisoned forever."

To which Barbara Tuchman in *A Distant Mirror* adds her comment: "By Constantine's gift, Christianity was both officially established and fatally compromised."[6] I think she puts it well. I hear in Tuchman's prose and Langland's poetry what I think is the effect of the third fall. The people of God, the church, is God's third attempt to create a community chosen to witness to the world what life under the sovereignty of God is like.

All these images—the sovereignty of God, the reign of God, the kingdom of God—are theological symbols for a possibility to be realized, a possibility never realized. It is realized eschatology: the kingdom is here, the kingdom is still to come. It is a faith statement about the dream of God.

The church is first of all a people called to live out that statement, not an institution. I believe that in the choice for Constantine, the institutional church rejected the call to be God's people.

There are three speeches in Dorothy Sayers's *Emperor Constantine* that foreshadow the church's accommodation to the culture as only the artist can—and they are particularly telling, since it was an artist who was interested in putting the best face on the whole affair. In the

first of those speeches, Constantine's sister says to his
wife:

> The lives of princes are not their own—they belong to
> the Empire. God's Empire first, and for the sake of that,
> to the Empire of the world. I am a Christian, wedded to
> a heathen husband—not by choice, yet willingly, if that
> may bring the Empire to Christ. Or if not, willingly all
> the same, since it might have been so, and it was right
> to try.[7]

In other words, anything goes—and we convince ourselves it is in the cause of the Lord. We live in the kingdoms of the world and convince ourselves we are only
doing it for the sake of the kingdom of God.

Later in the play, Constantine himself enunciates the
same idea, but now on a much larger scale. In this scene
he is receiving the bishops, who kiss his hand as they are
brought forward. Constantine says:

> I know that it grieves you all that I cannot, as yet, make
> myself wholly Christ's. But, as you are the Bishops of
> those within the Church, I am Bishop of those without,
> who have no shepherd and no High Priest but me. For
> a little longer I must needs be all things to all men.[8]

The church serves Constantine, and it has been blessing
his purposes and those of his imperial heirs ever since—
their wars, their social and economic arrangements, their
visions of the future. Life is divided into two orders, the
earthly and the heavenly; on earth, it is the business of
the heavenly to bless the earthly.

Gone are the days of the martyrs. Their only vestige is
in a third speech from Sayers's drama. It takes place during an imperial reception, and the Christian ladies of ele-
gance have been invited—only to the reception, not to
the dinner that preceded it. One of them, Paulina, smug

in her self-righteousness while enjoying all the benefits of her station, chides the others:

> Oh, you ladies take things so easily. You follow the fashion and sun yourselves in the Emperor's favour. But the evil days may return. There are martyrs in my family. This bone [she touches a reliquary at her neck] bore witness to Christ in the arena under Diocletian.[9]

Does a vision of all the crosses you have seen around the necks of the faithful come to your mind?

Paulina gets the response she wants. Another lady coos, "Dear Madam, you make us feel very humble."

How far the third fall has removed us from the dream of God!

As I reflect on the three falls, it seems to me they are not unconnected. First we human beings succumb to the temptation to be God, to know absolutely what is good and what is evil. Then we decide that the kingdoms of the world have more to offer than the kingdom of God. From there it is a very short distance to proclaiming the kingdoms of this world as the kingdom of God. For Constantine and his successors, the plan of God has been fulfilled. Beyond the present political order, all that Christians are to hope for is their own personal transference to the heavenly kingdom.

Jaroslav Pelikan, the distinguished historian, has written a handsome bestseller called *Jesus Through the Centuries*. He begins his chapter on the Constantinian influence with a quotation from the book of Revelation, "The kingdom of the world has become the kingdom of our Lord and his Christ." I respond to the beautiful quality of the language, but it is poetry and not prose. To turn poetry into prose exposes us to the temptation to settle for what is. It sets down as absolute reality the experience of one time, trying to make the language of metaphor the language of fact. Feminists struggle with this idea when they take exception to the metaphor of the kingdom of God, since it has been used, they say, to affirm a certain kind of power.

There is evidence in the gospels that Jesus resisted the title "king," and John records that when Pilate asked him directly, "Are you a king?", he refused to give him a direct answer. Jesus knew the only image the Hebrews had of a king was David, and the only image Pilate had was Caesar. Nevertheless, Pilate identified Jesus as a king on the cross, and that identification, says Pelikan, moved out into the world of nations and empires.

> Before the entire process of the enthronement of Jesus as King of Kings was finished, it had transformed the political life of a large part of the human race.... To trace the historical variations and permutations of the kingship of Jesus in its interaction with other political themes and symbols is to understand a large part of what is noble and a large part of what is demonic in the political history of the West.[10]

Christ reigning from the cross is a powerful symbol but in the triumphalism of the institutional church, we lose sight of the kind of king Jesus was. The rich priestly robes of the *Christus Rex* all but blot out the cruelty of the cross, and there is no room for the washbasin and towel of the Servant.

The earliest gospel records two incidents that foreshadow how hard it will be for his followers to understand Jesus' message. In Mark 8, Jesus and his disciples are on the road to Caesarea Philippi, and Jesus asks his disciples, "Who do people say that I am?" There is much

stumbling and bumbling on the disciples' part—they
wonder if he is a reincarnation of John the Baptist, or
Elijah, or one of the prophets. "But who do you say that
I am?" he asks pointedly, and Peter in a moment of inspiration replies, "You are the Christ." In other words, the
Hebrew Messiah, the long-awaited deliverer of the
Israelite nation, has come. When Jesus tells them what is
to happen to him, his rejection by the religious leaders
and his execution, Peter is appalled. There is no place in
his understanding for a Messiah who would die.

But Jesus is striving for a new understanding of
Messiah, of God's leader. Two chapters later, when they
are on the way to Jerusalem, Jesus again tells his disciples
what is going to happen in Jerusalem. Betrayal and condemnation, humiliation and death. Immediately James
and John ask him a favor: they want to sit in honored
places when he comes into his glory. Jesus says, "You do
not know what you are asking." And he was right. The
disciples saw a great battle and a triumphal procession for
the victor, with his favored lieutenants on his right hand
and on his left.

They were brave men. They foresaw a struggle, and
they were ready for it. When Jesus asked them, "Are you
able to drink the cup that I drink, or to be baptized with
the baptism with which I am baptized?", their bold
answer, "We are able," was no idle boast. They were pre-
pared to do battle in the kind of warfare they understood.
But they did not understand the new thing that Jesus was
about, and it has not become any clearer for the church
they founded. They did not understand Jesus' words:

> You know that those who are supposed to rule over the
> Gentiles lord it over them, and their great men exercise
> authority over them. But it shall not be so among you;
> but whoever would be great among you must be your

servant, and whoever would be first among you must be slave of all. (Mark 10:42b–44)

A totally new idea of kingship!

The early Christians died rather than accept Caesar's claim to be supreme king. Then the church was faced with the problem of Caesar becoming Christian.

Or did he?

Constantine's language in addressing bishops and clergy was properly deferential, but behind the deference was the firm hand of one who knew where the real power lay. The claim of Matthew's gospel that all authority in heaven and on earth had been given to the Risen Lord was transformed. Instead, authority was transmitted to the emperor, beginning with Constantine; Christ the King had elected to exercise his sovereignty through the emperor, to whom he appeared in visions. The emperor was crowned by God in the East, and he appointed the head of the church. At the consecration of the patriarch, the Byzantine emperor would declare, "By the grace of God and by our imperial power, which proceeds from the grace of God, this man is appointed patriarch of Constantinople."

In the time before time, God offered human creatures a way to live in harmony with themselves, with each other, and with all living things. This way of life required complete trust in God. Then we chose godhood for ourselves. We grasped at equality with God.

The first fall.

The biblical story says that God did not give up on this proud creature, but set out to call together a people to live as God's people and show the world another possibility for human life. Once again this entailed the risk of depending absolutely on God, and the chosen people chose the way of the kingdoms of the world. "Give us a king so that we can be like all the other nations."

The second fall.

Then the action of God—the way of God—became incarnate in a Nazarene carpenter, Jesus of Nazareth. He put his whole trust in God, above every structure, every system, and every loyalty. A free man, he loved, he taught, he showed another way. He so infused his followers with his spirit that even after he died they knew he lived, and the movement that he began swept on in power until it could no longer live in the uncertainties of trusting God. It became an institution, one among many, even if one over many.

The third fall.

1. Walter Brueggemann, *The Message of the Psalms* (Minneapolis: Augsburg, 1984), 36–38.
2. Bernard Anderson, *Understanding the Old Testament* (Englewood Cliffs, N.J.: Prentice-Hall, 1975), 136–137.
3. Roland Bainton, *The Church of Our Fathers* (Philadelphia: Westminster, 1950), 43.
4. Charles Williams, *Descent of the Dove* (London: Faber & Faber, 1945), 72.
5. Dorothy L. Sayers, *The Emperor Constantine* (New York: Harper & Bros., 1951), 25.
6. Barbara Tuchman, *A Distant Mirror* (New York: Knopf, 1984), 6.
7. Sayers, *Constantine*, 175.
8. Sayers, *Constantine*, 167.
9. Sayers, *Constantine*, 70.
10. Jaroslav Pelikan, *Jesus Through the Centuries* (New York: Yale University Press, 1985), 256.

Chapter Four

THE TEMPTATIONS
OF THE CHURCH

About halfway through *The Brothers Karamazov,* Dostoyevsky inserts the story of the Grand Inquisitor—a sequence, I think, that stands on its own as a classic indictment of the institutional church. The scene is set in Seville during the most terrible time of the Spanish Inquisition, when bonfires were lit every day to glorify God and burn wicked heretics. To these hot pavements Jesus comes again and moves among the people with healing, life-giving power. Then he is arrested by the Grand Inquisitor.

The Grand Inquisitor is a weary old man. When the day passes and is followed by the dark, burning, breathless night, he comes to the close, gloomy vaulted prison in the ancient palace of the Holy Inquisition. He stands in the doorway and for a minute or two gazes into the prisoner's face.

Is it Thou? Thou? Don't answer. Be silent. What canst thou say, indeed? I know too well what Thou wouldst say. And Thou hast no right to add anything to what Thou hast said of old. Why, then, art Thou come to hinder us? For Thou hast come to hinder us, and Thou knowest that.[1]

Everything has been given by Christ to the Pope, and all is therefore in the Pope's hands, and there is no need now for Jesus to come.

The Grand Inquisitor boasts that he and his church have banished freedom, and have done so to make men happy. "For the first time, it has become possible to think of the happiness of men. Man is created a rebel," he tells the prisoner, "and how can rebels be happy?"

"Instead of taking men's freedom," the Grand Inquisitor charges Jesus, "Thou didst make it greater than ever!" He continues:

> Didst Thou forget that man prefers peace, and even death, to freedom of choice in the knowledge of good and evil? Nothing is more seductive for man than his freedom of conscience, but nothing is a greater cause of suffering. Thou didst desire man's free love, that he should follow thee freely, be enticed and taken captive by Thee. In place of the rigid ancient law, man must hereafter with free heart decide for himself what is good and what is evil, having only Thy image before him as his guide.

When Jesus rejected miracle, mystery, and authority, which is how Dostoyevsky interprets his temptations in the wilderness, then he laid the foundation for the destruction of his own kingdom and no one else is more to blame for it. The church, the Grand Inquisitor proudly declares, corrected Jesus' mistake and founded the church on these same three temptations—miracle, mystery, and authority.

And to the silent prisoner, he says, "And why dost Thou look silently and searchingly at me with Thy mild eyes? Be angry. I don't want Thy love, for I love Thee not."

Jesus of Nazareth is a troubling—and troublesome—figure, and it seems to me the church has never known what to do with him.

As I interpret the biblical story, the heart of the relationship between God and human beings is freedom. Freedom is the image of God in the human creature. God freely chose to create. God did not have to create the world, for God would be God without the world. I do not think these are esoteric assertions, the meat of irrelevant theological disputes. I think they are at the heart of the biblical understanding of God. A lonely God, a vulnerable God, a God who loves.

Love is not the only way to be in relationship. There are other ways: master-slave, leader-follower, doctor-patient, expert-beneficiary, helper-helped, parent-child. None of these relationships necessarily involves love. God chose a relationship that involved love—lover-beloved—and was utterly devoid of coercion. Love has to be freely given and must be freely received.

Out of my freedom, I choose to love you. Out of your freedom, you can reject my love. That awesome freedom, the Grand Inquisitor—for me, the institutional church—rejects.

It is comforting for the church to declare the Bible the Word of God instead of taking seriously what the Bible says—that Jesus himself is the Word of God. It is troubling to consider that God did not become incarnate as a book, but as a person.

Books are records that can be sealed in time. They show how the writer saw it at one time. If writers change their minds, they have to write another book. How many books they can write is limited by, among other things, how long they live. After their deaths, the interpretation of what they wrote is left to succeeding generations, who may or may not correctly interpret the original writer.

Endless possibilities for chaos loom, so in the case of the Holy Word, the institutional church stepped in, decided what the record meant, and devised heresy as a means of protecting its interpretation. "Thou hast no right to add anything," the Grand Inquisitor says. The church has banished freedom.

How troubling that God came as a person and not a book! And if that Person is eternally living, eternally in communication with God's people, one age can eternally say to another, "Your understanding is not my understanding. God has a new word to say to us."

Dostoyevsky deals insightfully in his novel with the temptation stories, following the order given in Matthew. Jesus rejects the temptation to carry out his mission by miracle (turning the stones into bread); by mystery (special treatment for God's special ones); and by the exercise of power (responding as the kingdoms of this world respond). The Grand Inquisitor deems Jesus' choice a mistake, and proudly declares the church corrected the mistake and established the church on the very foundations rejected by Jesus. The way the church has treated the resurrection is the classic example of this. A profound act of God (calling for a response in faith and courage) has been declared a miraculous historical event to which everyone must respond in the same way, despite the lack of unanimity about the event in the biblical record itself.

"There is no nostalgia in the New Testament," Tad Dunne writes.

There is no evidence even in post-testamental literature that anyone enshrined Jesus' clothes, let alone stashed the shroud for the sake of the faith. The reason, of course, is that Christians believed that Jesus was present to them in a far more important and vital way. Resurrection faith does not believe that Jesus "came back" to life in the manner Lazarus did. Rather it believes that the Father "lifted up" Jesus after He died, giving Him a new kind of life, a life by which He could be present to any disciple anywhere, as evidenced by the post-Resurrection appearances. People interested in remnants of the past usually feel something has been lost, but Jesus has not been lost to Christians with the Resurrection faith. Still, there is the question, "What really happened at the tomb?" No New Testament writer seems to care. Their question was rather, "What is God about to do?"[2]

The crucifixion was an historical event. All four gospels report the arrest, the hasty trial, the condemnation, the execution, and the death—all events in time. The earliest gospel reports that women were the first witnesses of the resurrection, and their response was fear. In Luke, intimate friends of Jesus going home from Jerusalem have an experience that lets them know he is alive, and they rush back to tell the other members of the community. In a little Pentecost in John's gospel, the disciples, huddled fearfully behind closed doors, are visited by the Risen Lord. Magdalene, weeping disconsolately in the garden, has her own experience of not being alone. Peter, wretched at the memory of his denial, has his own experience of forgiveness. The power of the resurrection goes on. Paul, who never knew Jesus in the flesh, encounters him in a life-changing experience.

The resurrection is the experience of knowing whom we believe—"knowing" in the biblical sense, which is participating in the life, and believing in the biblical sense, which is risking our lives that God is for us. That faith cannot be organized, systematized, or institutional-ized.

Raymond Brown, the Roman Catholic scholar of the New Testament who has been honored by a pope for his loyalty to the teaching of the church, says in *The Churches the Apostles Left Behind*, "The great anomaly of Christianity is that only through an institution can the message of a non-institutional Jesus be preserved."[3] Jesus came proclaiming, "Repent! The kingdom of God is at hand." His message was, "Turn around! You are going in the wrong direction. You have been seduced by the ways of the kingdoms of the world. I offer you the way of life in the kingdom of God."

That message cannot be institutionalized because its very essence is freedom. In the kingdom of God, each moment calls for decision. What I so surely knew to be right yesterday, today I may find to be wrong.

How hard it is for individuals to admit an error in judgment or perception or action! How much harder—almost impossible—it is for institutions, where systems and strategies are already in place. And yet the church is called to such an impossibility. What is impossible with human beings is possible with God.

The danger that the institution must always wrestle with, however, is that the message may be altered to fit the purposes of the institution. A friend of mine, reflecting on this quandary, observed that institutions come into being to preserve an idea. As long as it is doing its job well, the institution is unimportant. If the institution is failing to do its job, that is when it becomes important to preserve the institution.

I can glimpse this movement in the transition from the tumultuous freedom of the Spirit in Paul's letters to the little communities gathered for worship in Corinth and Rome to the overriding concern for discipline and order we see later on in the pastoral epistles, 1 and 2 Timothy and Titus. In Paul's letters there is imagination and poetry and passion as he tries to work out for the little communities what new thing God is doing with them. He calls on the image of the body to show that gifts differ but service is one, and all the gifts are equally valuable.

The church of Timothy and Titus, by contrast, has well-defined orders of bishops and deacons; indeed, the letters were written for these leaders. In his letter to the Philippians, Paul had expressed tender concern for Euodia and Syntyche, whom he knew personally; in the pastoral letters, women are to be managed and controlled lest by their exuberance they upset a stabilized group. Paul struggles in his letter to the Romans to give them his understanding of the freedom from the law God has given in Christ Jesus, and his words tumble over each other as he concludes with that organ roll of faith, "If God be for us, who can be against us?" Later on, there is no need to wrestle with questions of doctrine, but to declare it with authority and weed out the dissidents.

William Clebsch, one of the young radicals who founded the Episcopal Seminary of the Southwest in Austin, Texas, warned that "faith in order to be incarnate must risk becoming a religion, but religion is always in danger of murdering faith." It is the dilemma of incarnation.

"Institutions are necessary," said a friend of mine who was contemplating the development of another institution, a consortium of Protestant and Roman Catholic seminaries organized to take seriously the ministry of the laity their graduates were to serve, but he admitted, "embodiment does something to the vision."

"Loses it," I suggested.

"What does that say about the Incarnation?" he asked.

I understood then the power of Colossians 2:9, where the author of the letter is stressing the uniqueness of Jesus Christ as opposed to philosophical concepts about the elemental spirits of the universe: "For in him the whole fulness of deity dwells bodily." Jesus was the fullness of the godhead bodily—he was not the whole of God, only that part of God which could be contained in a body. That is where the church has gone astray—equating Jesus with the fullness of God, making Jesus an object of worship, rather than an expression of God to be followed.

The beginning of J. B. Phillips's translation of John's gospel reads:

> At the beginning God expressed himself. That personal expression, that word, was with God, and was God, and he existed with God from the beginning.[4]

I think we are dealing here with the central paradox of the Christian faith. Jesus was God. Jesus was not God.

I have heard it was St. Augustine who claimed the doctrine of the Trinity was said in order that it might not be left unsaid. That seems to me to be a good way to approach it. The question that the Trinity is trying to express is beyond the scope of reason. The hymnist expresses it well for me:

> I know not how that Bethlehem's babe
> Could in the Godhead be;
> I only know the manger child
> Has brought God's life to me.

I know not how that Joseph's tomb
Could solve death's mystery;
I only know a living Christ,
Our immortality.

The raw material of faith is not fact but experience. It is not what your mind, by a series of rational steps, tells you is so. Faith is what your experience, in a way you cannot explain to someone else's satisfaction, gives you the courage to risk.

Dostoyevsky's Grand Inquisitor understood that Jesus wanted human beings to decide freely for themselves what is good and what is evil, having only the life of Jesus before them as a guide. Institutions prefer the safety and security of "rigid ancient law."

It is the resurrection that speaks more about the totality of God than the earthly Jesus, but the institution quickly tamed the resurrection and set the earthly Jesus as an object of worship.

A book entitled *From Jesus to Christ* is one historian's search to find out how the messenger became the message. Its author, Paula Fredrikson, argues that there is an historical gap between the apostles' experience of the resurrection and their proclamation of it. There are no direct sources for what went on in the life of that community from the hour they knew that the death on Calvary had not defeated God until they had a well-defined message to preach: God has come in Jesus of Nazareth and God will come again. As a message it was overwhelmingly successful, but Fredrikson believes the delay of the Second Coming necessitated an adjustment in the message, one that took Jesus' followers away from the man who first called them to a religion *about* this man.

Jesus did not come to bring a new religion. As religions go, Judaism was as good as any, and Jesus practiced it up to the end:

> That last night at supper lying
> Mid the twelve, his chosen band,
> Jesus, with the Law complying,
> Keeps the feast its rites demand.

Religion is always "about" God: intellectual formulations, institutional orderings, liturgical expressions. All, over time, run the danger of solidifying into "God." Instead, Jesus came as the Way, a new possibility for encountering God ever anew in the fluid, changing experience of life.

Who was this Jesus, and what was he about? I believe Jesus is the Word made flesh, the definitive action of God for our age to offer human beings a new possibility for participating in the dream of God, and the Christian church is missing the mark. The church missed its high calling to be the new thing in the world when it decided to worship Jesus instead of follow him. We live in a day when it would be equally offensive to those who bear the name of Christian to hear Jesus blasphemed as to see him followed. And yet discipleship, not worship, is what Jesus called for.

To the rich man who ran up and knelt before him, asking, "Good Teacher, what must I do to inherit eternal life?", Jesus replied promptly, "Why do you call me good? No one is good but God alone." To the woman who cried out to him, "Blessed is the womb that bore you, and the breasts that you sucked!" Jesus replied, "Blessed rather are those who hear the word of God and keep it!"

Jesus did not call human beings to worship him, but to follow him.

Worship is setting Jesus on a pedestal, distancing him, enshrining (enshrouding) him in liturgies, stained glass windows, biblical translations, medallions, pilgrimages to places where he walked—the whole nine yards. Following him is doing what he did, weeping over a situation that was so far removed from the dream of God and spending his life to make it different. Following is discipleship.

In the first sermon of Jesus of which we have a record (Luke 4:18–19), Jesus takes note of the fact that the world is not as God would have it be and he has come to restore it to what God wants. The poor will hear good news, the captives will be freed, the blind will receive sight, the oppressed will be liberated. The world will be released from its bondage to Satan.

Jesus saw himself as in a titanic struggle with the powers of evil. When his opponents accused him of being in league with the prince of demons, he pointed out how ridiculous such an idea was. "A kingdom divided against itself cannot stand," he said. "Why would I be acting against Satan if I am in the service of Satan?"

Following Jesus is having that clear-eyed vision of whom we serve. Worship, unless it is in the service of discipleship—and when it is, it is a very different thing from what is going on in most of the churches—is blasphemy.

At the turn of the twentieth century a battle was waged in church circles between the proponents of the Jesus of history and the proponents of the Christ of the church. The idea was that there had been a simple Galilean carpenter going around doing good, who was the Jesus of history, and after that a construct, generally attributed to St. Paul, which was the Christ of the church. Then Albert Schweitzer wrote his definitive book *The Quest of*

the Historical Jesus, with its compelling thesis that there was no way to recapture the historical Jesus, that the very records we would use to do so were themselves the polemical faith statements of the church. All we have is the Christ of the church.

In recent decades there have been three challenges to Schweitzer's thesis, and all from within the Roman Catholic Church. The first is from a Dominican scholar, Albert Nolan, in a book with the provocative title *Jesus Before Christianity*. The second challenge is from a professor of philosophy at Loyola University, Thomas Sheehan, in his book *The First Coming*, while the third is by another Dominican, Lucas Grollenberg's *The Unexpected Messiah*. Even the subtitles Sheehan and Grollenberg give their books are instructive: Sheehan's is *How the Kingdom of God Became Christianity*, and Grollenberg's is *How the Bible Can Be Misleading*.

Together these books make three points. First, Jesus of Nazareth has been lost in the Christ of the institutional church. Jesus of Nazareth is to be followed; the Christ of the church is to be worshiped. Second, the community gathered in Jesus' name lost Jesus' vision in the century after his death, and the institutional church conforms more to its own distorted heritage than to Jesus of Nazareth. Third, a literalist reading of the New Testament can end up scapegoating the Jews and absolving the rest of us of our failure to follow Jesus. Our failures are always to be found in ourselves, not in any incident of history. God's call is always present for us either to accept or reject.

The first book, the simplest and easiest to read, is possibly the most disconcerting of them all. Nolan claims that Jesus of Nazareth faced a situation similar to ours, the prospect of an unparalleled catastrophe, and he believes the similarity of the two situations provides us with a new perspective on Jesus. Many people have understood that Jesus' ministry must be seen in the light of an impending crisis; both he and John the Baptist foresaw the destruction of the world as they knew it. Many commentators before Nolan have read Jesus' message as apocalyptic—prepare to meet your God, who is coming on the clouds to judge the world and rescue the righteous—but Nolan thinks Jesus' message is, God has come and offered us another way to live.

The ultimate question is the meaning of human existence. Are we free creatures who can choose to work with a loving Creator to restore a good creation? Or are we miserable creatures in a scenario that is nasty, brutish, and short, living in an adversarial relationship with a menacing God, with our only hope to be strong enough to grab what we can in this life or compliant enough to secure a good place in the next? The prophets took their stand with the first alternative. They kept the dialogue going between Creator and creatures because they had hope for history. The apocalyptic writers were without hope—this world was lost, and the only thing to do was prepare for the next, where, incidentally, there were only so many places.

Nolan sees the driving force for Jesus, the source from which all his actions came, as compassion. Jesus chose to identify with the poor and oppressed, Nolan says. He was not born poor, but in the middle class, and he became an outcast by choice. His only motive for healing people was compassion, but he never thought he had a monopoly on compassion and faith. What he wanted was to awaken the same compassion and faith in the people around him, and enable them to receive and exercise God's power.

The good news Jesus preached was the good news of the kingdom of God, a reality that was already among them. "The kingdom of God is in your midst," he said. To change his words to "The kingdom of God is in you" is a notorious mistranslation that individualizes and spiritualizes the kingdom of God, so that it is no longer a threat to the kingdoms of this world. Jesus enunciated and lived out the values of the kingdom of God instead of the values of the kingdoms of the world in the realms of money, prestige, human solidarity, power, time—and the choice for the kingdom of God.

He asked for a total and general sharing of all possessions. The kingdom of God will be a society in which there will be no prestige and no status, no division of people into inferior and superior. Everybody will be loved and respected, not because of education or wealth or ancestry or authority or rank or virtue or achievements, but because each human being is created by God and loved by God. Jesus understood love as solidarity. Love your enemies, and call them enemies no more.

Faith is a straightforward decision for the kingdom of God. To believe in God is to believe that goodness is more powerful than evil and truth is stronger than falsehood. To believe in God is to believe that in the end goodness and truth will triumph over evil and falsehood. "If Jesus had not believed that," Nolan writes, "he would have had nothing at all to say."[5]

This kind of believing, however, brought him into direct confrontation with the powers that be, and the last third of Nolan's book is called "Confrontation." He ends on the question of what it means to say we believe in Jesus:

> The beginning of faith in Jesus is the attempt to read the signs of our times as Jesus read the signs of his times, to recognize that all the forces working against humankind are the forces of evil, and to believe as Jesus did that every form of evil can be overcome.[6]

If this is what Jesus was all about, how did the community gathered in his name get so far off the mark? There is little difference between the values of the king-

doms of the world regarding money, prestige, human solidarity, and power, and the values of the church.
Acquisition of material wealth, the bid for status, the
fracturing of community, and the struggle for control
mark the life of the institutional church as they mark any
other institution.

This is the question to which my second book on Jesus,
Thomas Sheehan's *The First Coming*, proposes an answer:
how did the people of God, the Christian church, move
from God-with-man to God-with-one-man, from "Thy
kingdom come" to "Come, Lord Jesus"? Jesus came to
show us what we all could become, but we made him so
special no one else could be like him. He lived in the
power of the kingdom come, but we live in the expectation of a beyond-time event.

How did the church come to see Jesus as someone we
can only worship in awe, rather than follow in his footsteps? Why did we have to make him so different from
the rest of us that his experiences have no relevance for
our daily life—working in the structures of society, being
a parent, a sibling, a friend, being sad and glad, discour-
aged or confused, being insignificantly human? How did
we put his announcement of the present reality of the
kingdom into a formula we rattle off without meaning it,
and turn instead to chanting "Come, Lord Jesus" as if we
were calling for an event that has not yet happened?
What if we have misunderstood Jesus?

The important question to ask is not "What do you
believe?" but "What difference does it make that you
believe?" Does the world come nearer to the dream of
God because of what you believe?

In a learned and compelling manner, Sheehan traces the process by which we have come to pay more attention to Jesus himself than to the message he preached, and he reminds us that Jesus is not the object of his message: "The proclaimer of the kingdom gives way to the reality he preached."[7] After describing the turbulent background against which we have to understand Jesus' ministry, Sheehan moves on to the narratives of crucifixion and resurrection. The real shock for orthodoxy lies in Simon Peter's experience and the empty tomb. The "Easter experience" is the experience of forgiveness, and Simon Peter came to understand that the real denial of Jesus lay in holding on to Jesus himself and thereby forgetting what he was about.

Jesus had tried to prepare his disciples for the fact that his way would lead to death, because the kingdoms of the world would not permit the kind of challenge he represented. The disciples could not grasp this fact; even though they had experienced the destruction of prophets, they could not accept the fact it would also happen to Jesus.

"The scandal of those last days in Jerusalem," Sheehan insists, "was not that Jesus was crucified, but that the disciples lost faith in what he had proclaimed. Jesus' every word had been a promise of life, but they fled when threatened with death. He had trusted utterly in God; but they feared men."[8]

Sheehan imagines Peter reflecting on that fact. He remembered his denial. Sheehan connects that with Peter's experience on the storm-tossed sea, as Peter remembered that death and life experience: "Save us, Lord, we're going under." In the dark days after Jesus' death, Peter had an insight, a revelatory experience, his Easter experience of the Father's forgiveness. In his dark despair, he felt the Father's forgiveness as the experience of a drowning man pulled from the bottom of the sea.

Like Nolan, Sheehan understands that the ethic of the kingdom, compassion, entailed always taking the side of the weaker or disadvantaged party and therefore the side of the poor and the oppressed—including those whom the religious establishment declared to be outcasts.

If the Father was henceforth to be identified with human beings, Sheehan argues,

> that is, if the kingdom of God was at hand, then strictly speaking there was no longer a God-up-above upon whom one could make religious claims by scrupulously observing the Law. In that sense, the demands of mercy that Jesus made were more rigorous than the stipulation of the Law. In calling for the commitment of the whole person to the immediate presence of the Father, Jesus necessarily pointed that commitment in the direction of one's fellow human beings, especially the socially powerless and disenfranchised.[9]

If we ask about the timing of this eschatological event, that is, *when* God's kingdom was supposed to arrive, we are faced with an apparent contradiction. According to what Jesus preached, the reign of God-with-man at one and the same time had already arrived in the present and yet was still to come in the future. This paradox of the simultaneous presence and futurity of God's kingdom, Sheehan understands as the core of Jesus' message: the eschatological present-future. Like Nolan, Sheehan sees forgiveness as crucial to Jesus' message:

> Apocalyptic imagery was no longer needed because the eschatological line between the age of sin and the age of grace was already being crossed. God was now with God's people. We do not have to look for God to do

anything else. God has already done it all. It is now up
to God's people to live out that forgiven life.[10]

The name Jesus used for this passing of the ages, says
Sheehan, was forgiveness.

> Forgiveness, as Jesus preached it, referred not primarily
> to sin at all, but the crossing of the eschatological line.
> What was given in the Father's forgiveness was the
> eschatological future, that is, God. Thus forgiveness
> meant the arrival of God in the present, God's super-
> abundant gift of God to God's people, God's self-commu-
> nicating incarnation.[11]

In Jesus' preaching, the giving of this forgiveness was
entirely the initiative of God. And yet at the same time
it was not an objective event that God dropped out of
the sky. God became present when people allowed that
presence by actualizing it in lives of justice and charity.
The promise of eschatology was converted into the
demand for love and justice.

Sheehan concludes by charging Christianity with dis-
torting the message of Jesus, whom he consistently refers
to as the prophet, in three ways. First of all, the church
committed the sin of idolatry by turning what Jesus was
about into Jesus himself. Jesus preached God with all
people, not just the special ones. Christianity preached
God with one person, Jesus, and whoever calls on his
name will be saved.

Second, Christianity abandoned Jesus' radical sense of
time. It surrendered the present-future for a mythical
past-present-future, a "salvation history," according to
which God had become man in the past, was now reigning in heaven, and would return to the earth in the
future.

Third, it reconstituted religion by setting up a new
object of worship. Sheehan says Jesus did not undertake

his prophetic mission to bring people more religion (surely there was enough already) or a different religion (Judaism was quite adequate) or the true and perfect religion, which is a contradiction in terms. Jesus came to define the kingdom of God by the way he lived.

> He concretely enacted the kingdom in the table fellowship that he shared with his followers, in the parables that he told them, and in the "signs and wonders" that he worked among the people.[12]

The challenge of my third author, Lucas Grollenberg, arose out of his concern over what Christianity had done to Judaism. The plan for his book, Grollenberg says, came about as a result of feelings of irritation and amazement during a church service one year shortly before Christmas. The celebrant sang solemnly about Christ, whose coming "prophets foresaw and prophesied." That irritated Grollenberg, for it implies that the Jews must have been hard of heart and blind to reject a Messiah who was so clearly prophesied in their own Bible. He remembered two splendid female statues that adorn the south porch of Strasbourg Cathedral. One represents the synagogue, with a blindfold over her eyes, a broken staff in one hand and in the other a law book she is almost dropping. Over against her stands the church with a triumphant look on her face, a crown on her head, bearing a chalice in her left hand and proudly holding out before her a cross in her right hand.

Grollenberg devotes much time and space to the historical situation in which Jesus lived. He argues that Jesus was conditioned by his environment, making the

THE DREAM OF GOD

telling and winsome analogy that Mozart did not spring full-blown as a musician out of nowhere—music was all around him. Jesus, says Grollenberg, emerged from a people who, unlike the pagans, depended on one particular religion.

He minimizes Jewish responsibility for Jesus' death, and emphasizes instead that the power which killed Jesus was imperial Rome. At the time of Pilate, Caiaphas, and Herod Antipas in Galilee, a charismatic leader who drew crowds could count on being executed—excited crowds threatened the law and order that the Romans and their functionaries wanted to maintain at any price.

Then Grollenberg considers the anti-Jewish thrust of New Testament scriptures, carefully analyzes what they meant then, and seriously questions their value for today. The Bible must always be read in its historical context, and to set up any part of the Bible as the absolute truth for all time is to make it into an idol. He quotes a Jewish scholar who believes that although a Christian can only regret that such "anti-Jewish" texts came into being and began to circulate within the movement of a man who preached love, especially love toward enemies, nevertheless the expressions are understandable. It is a universal phenomenon that we are seldom generous toward rivals; when we supplant them, we try to show that they did not deserve their status and that they are worse than we are. He is also generous to recall a similar attitude in the Hebrew Bible, where the adherents of other religions are often mocked. (Isaiah 44, for instance, is a parody, and no Babylonian would have recognized himself in it.) Furthermore, the people who are depicted in such a negative way in the New Testament no longer exist, but those texts, read time and again as words of God, have had the power to keep alive and nurture the hatred of Jews in Christian societies, with abhorrent consequences in every century.

84

Finally, Grollenberg turns to what Jesus had to say about the coming kingdom of God. He believes that an authentic saying of Jesus about destroying the Temple and raising it up in three days has been preserved in the various versions we have. For Jesus, Grollenberg says, God's dearest wish for humankind was very clear. It was not just a matter of avoiding murder, theft, adultery, false witness, and other such crimes. What God really wanted had to be expressed in much more radical terms: real love toward all fellow men and women. Jesus put that briefly and powerfully in the so-called golden rule: "Whatever you want others to do to you, do so to them." The coming kingdom of God was to consist of a community of people who would find one another in love. The few times that Jesus refers to the future, he uses images like a wedding or a banquet; that is how the Father wanted to associate with his children. A temple would no longer be necessary. Grollenberg writes:

> It was not unusual in the time of Jesus for a close community of people dedicated to God to be called a temple. We know that from the writings of the Essenes who lived by the Dead Sea. They spoke of their group not only as the "community of the new covenant," but also as "the temple of God."[13]

Jesus' saying could be understood in that sense: the Temple of Jerusalem will no longer have a function, but will disappear. After three days, which is the usual time for a change for the better, God will put a new one in its place, a community of fulfilled people.

Whatever happened to the dream? Is the company of fulfilled people the end goal of God's creating activity?

Paul Hanson in *The People Called* boldly sets forth as the underlying presupposition and method of his biblical theology the belief that "since the world's beginning, God has been active in fidelity to a creative, redemptive purpose, and will remain active until this world has completed its divinely ordained intention."[14] He goes on to say that purpose has included fellowship with the human family, a fellowship arising out of confession of God's sovereignty and expressing itself in gratitude and praise. The fulfilled people will live out the life of the kingdom of God, God's divinely ordained creation, expressed in such biblical images as "thy kingdom come, thy will be done on earth," the Holy City coming down out of heaven to earth, and the acceptable year of the Lord.

Earlier, I castigated the church for its surrender to Constantine, but you may remember I also said that the problems of institutionalization began with the New Testament churches. These churches made the choice against freedom, and opted instead for institutionalization—doctrine, order, and control. In the process, I believe, they lost the free man Jesus and what he was about.

Of course there were reasons for the choice, good reasons as well as bad. The Christians had entered the second stage of development, the missionary stage was over, and the organizational stage had begun. All these little communities were scattered about the ancient world, preaching a new gospel about what God wanted for the world and how God had acted to bring a dream into being. But these churches were not the only source of religious ferment in the world at that time. There were ecstasies that were older than theirs, and their very fervor spawned many other forms in their midst. So there had to be some clarity established, some lines drawn, and some safeguards placed on the apostolic teaching. The whole enterprise had to be organized, ordered, and controlled or it might be lost.

The tradition might well have remembered a salutary word from Jesus on this point: "He who finds his life will lose it, and he who loses his life for my sake will find it." Institutions are not good at losing their lives.

In *The Churches the Apostles Left Behind*, Raymond Brown details the legacy of the apostles in seven New Testament records: the Pauline heritage in the pastoral epistles, in Colossians and Ephesians, and in Luke / Acts; the Petrine heritage in 1 Peter; the heritage of John (whom he consistently calls the Beloved Disciple as a more accurate designation, because the identity of the disciple whom Jesus loved is unknown to us and was probably not one of the Twelve); and finally, the heritage of the Jewish / Gentile community in Matthew.

Paul's heritage was church structure. He used the great image of the church, the people of God, as a body, "the body of Christ." Paul details the gifts: apostles, prophets, teachers, workers of miracles, healers, helpers, administrators, speakers in various kinds of tongues. The pastoral letters soberly organize the roles: bishops, deacons, elders.

Paul's image of the body of Christ also appears in Colossians and Ephesians with much more exalted language and excitement. The church achieves a semidivine character, almost beyond reproach. The church is his body, "the fulness of him who fills all in all."

The heritage of Peter was the church as the people of God, as evidenced in 1 Peter: "Once you were no people but now you are God's people" (2:10). This community was largely composed of Gentile converts and was in danger of severe persecutions. They may have had occasion to wonder why they had gotten embroiled in this Jewish business, anyway. Peter assures them their claim to membership in the people of God is sure.

The heritage of the Beloved Disciple is a community guided by the Spirit. The Spirit is comforter and teacher, and each one has equal access to the Spirit. There are no second-class citizens. Finally, Matthew's heritage of the Jewish / Gentile community was authority that had been personalized in Jesus through statements like, "You have heard it said of old, but I say unto you. . . ."

These are the ideas left to us by the early churches: the importance of church structure; the church as a community, corporate but not institutional; the movement of the Spirit; the people of God; the necessity for a personal relationship to Jesus; and a high respect for law and authority.

There was—and still is—cost and promise in all of this, and Brown does not flinch from naming the costs. The idea of preserving the apostolic heritage against radical ideas runs into the great danger of the exclusive stress on officially controlled teaching, introduced at moments of crisis, becoming a consistent way of life. The safe institutional virtues required of pastors favor blandness. A sharp distinction between those who teach and those who learn—the statement "I permit no woman to teach" is particularly offensive to me—ignores the fact that teaching and learning go back and forth. It reminds me of Kipling's doggerel:

> The strength of the wolf is the pack,
> And the strength of the pack is the wolf.

Brown also has difficulty with the idea of separating the church as institution from the church as the people of God, but he admits, "It would be a sociological miracle if the Church as institution patterned on surrounding institutions would not be tempted to take over the values of money and power, the values of the world."[15]

The idea of the church as the people of God from the Petrine heritage makes for a strong sense of belonging among its members, but its weakness is that it fosters exclusivity. "We Christians," says Brown, "have never developed a satisfactory way of reconciling God's unique gift of grace through Christ and God's merciful love for all."[16]

The biblical status of the people of God reduces all others to a non-people. How many times have we heard, "What's going to happen to all those people who never heard about Jesus?" Letting everybody hear is the motivating force of the missionary movement—don't let those heathens in their blindness bow down to wood and stone. Teach them to bow down before western civilization and capitalism. Or teach them to read the Bible while the rear guard of the missionaries take their land, as Desmond Tutu put it. How easily our evangelistic efforts become doing something for the benighted in order to bring them up to our favored status.

We are first. They are below us. It is the issue of prestige, an issue Jesus dealt with by reversing the usual ideas of importance:

> Unless you turn and become like children, you will never enter the kingdom of heaven. (Matthew 18:3)

> For which is greater, one who sits at table, or one who serves? Is it not the one who sits at table? But I am among you as one who serves. (Luke 22:27)

The strength of an individual relationship to Jesus, which is the heritage of the Beloved Disciple, has in our day degenerated into the "me-and-Jesus" syndrome, an exaggerated form of Christian individualism.

After I had once offered as a discipline to a Christian group that they read the Bible and *The New York Times* together, a very earnest young woman in the group later told me with much excitement of a discipline she had developed with her prayer group. They "prayed" the daily paper. "How does that work?" I asked. She said they read the obituary columns and prayed for the deceased and their families; the bridal notices and asked blessings for the members of the wedding; the sports pages and lifted up to God those who would win and those who would lose. "What about the front pages? The editorials?" I asked. She was stunned—the fact that God was involved in more than the personal and the private was a new idea to her. For her the systems of the world lay outside the purview of God.

Simplistic religion like this cannot equip us to deal with the powers and principalities. A very talented young politician developed a winning strategy of negative campaigning. Months later he was stricken by a fatal illness. Preparing to meet his God, he repented of all the harm he had done to individuals and reached out to them in apology. Yet he apparently gave no thought to the systemic harm he had wrought by causing a political process to be derailed.

The Beloved Disciple's great gift of guidance by the Spirit lends itself to divisiveness. In our time we have seen the word "charismatic" become the exclusive property of one response to the Spirit, and congregations have been torn asunder, each side impugning the religious faith of the other.

Finally, the high respect for authority then and now divides us in church polemics. Who speaks for God? The Pope? The bishop? The congregational leaders? The individual? Brown, like Grollenberg, closes his book with a plea for a better use of the Bible:

I contend that in a divided Christianity, instead of reading the Bible to assure that we are right, we would do better to read it to discover where we have not been listening. . . . Then the Bible would be doing for us what Jesus did in his time, namely, convincing those who have ears to hear that all is not right, for God is asking of them more than they thought.[17]

His concern is ecumenical dialogue, but it speaks to me of the institutional church in any form—structured, as the liturgical churches are, or free-form, as the so-called free churches are. I believe that the church, in whatever form it appears institutionally, rejects the dream of God. The paradox is that within that institution the dream is kept; if it weren't, I would not be sharing my understanding and you would not be reading it. Or, in the words of a limerick recently given me by a friend:

O God, for as much as without thee,
We would not be able to doubt thee,
Give us the grace
To tell the whole race
It knows very little about thee.

1. Fyodor Dostoyevsky, *The Brothers Karamazov* (New York: The Modern Library, n.d.), 259–266.
2. Quoted in *Context* (October 1988): 3.
3. Raymond E. Brown, *The Churches the Apostles Left Behind* (New York: Paulist Press, 1984), 145.
4. J. B. Phillips, *The New Testament in Modern English* (London: Geoffrey Bles, 1960), 181.

5. Albert Nolan, *Jesus Before Christianity* (Maryknoll, N.Y.: Orbis Books, 1978), 85.
6. Nolan, *Jesus,* 140.
7. Thomas Sheehan, *The First Coming* (New York: Random House, 1986), 190, 218.
8. Sheehan, *First Coming,* 122–124.
9. Sheehan, *First Coming,* 59.
10. Sheehan, *First Coming,* 66–67.
11. Sheehan, *First Coming,* 69.
12. Sheehan, *First Coming,* 221–222.
13. Lucas Grollenberg, *The Unexpected Messiah* (London: SCM Press, 1987), 174.
14. Paul Hanson, *The People Called* (San Francisco: Harper & Row, 1986), 524.
15. Brown, *Churches,* 55.
16. Brown, *Churches,* 82.
17. Brown, *Churches,* 150.

Chapter Five

THE PERSISTENCE
OF THE DREAM

One of the carols written in the nineteenth century contains the sobering lines, "Beneath the angel strains have rolled / Two thousand years of wrong." The syndicated columnist William Raspberry once reported on a survey of America's brightest young people and found what he called "a rising tide of materialism." The survey indicated that incoming college students, traditionally a hotbed of youthful idealism, are overwhelmingly materialistic, interested primarily in making money. About the same time *The Washington Post* reported the findings of a Roman Catholic archbishop, who revealed that American Catholics are so individualistic it is difficult to preach economic justice to them. All this in a country where churches are found on every street corner.

What does religion mean in this country? Another columnist, Henry Mitchell, did a devastating take-off called "Spiritual Revival, 1980s Style," in which he explained that "more Americans go to more churches than is general in Europe. That's all [spiritual revival] really means. Except I would call it a church attendance revival, to be accurate." Mitchell went on to say that churchgoing and the spiritual life had more to do with affluence and upward mobility than the traditional hall-marks of the spiritual life such as self-denial, humility, and compassion. And if today

> the spiritual life means superiority to street people, a goal of upward mobility, and a general sense of having made it, thank God, then you can see that this spiritu-ality is no different from what used to be called the world, the flesh, and the devil.[1]

It is a long way from what Jesus was about.

I believe that the genius of Christianity is not creed or institution, but the vision of a new possibility for human life rooted in an ancient understanding of God, and articulated and lived out by a Nazarene carpenter from that tradition.

Will Campbell, a Mississippi native and a preacher of another stripe, quoting the great classical scholar Edith Hamilton from her book *Witness to the Truth*, said, "The fathers of the Church were good men, often saintly men, sometimes men who cared enough for Christ to die for him, but they did not trust him." They could not trust the safety of the church to his way of doing things, "so they set out to make the church safe in their own way." Like Edith Hamilton, Campbell believes that "the great church of Christ came into being ignoring the life of Christ."[2]

And so while Jesus preached repentance, the church settled for moralism. Repentance calls us all to acknowl-edge that we have done those things we ought not to have done, and we have not done those things we ought to have done, while moralism decides what is good and what is bad.

Moralism decides it is not good to kill fetuses, but it is not bad to kill grown men and women in state executions. Moralism decides praying in public is a good thing, so a denominational newspaper expresses admiration for businessmen praying aloud before lunch in a restaurant. One of the number became a United States senator who has voted for every military package presented to Congress. Moralism decides it is bad for young people to be exposed to dangerous books that attack traditional values, so *Hamlet*, *Wuthering Heights*, *The Red Badge of Courage*, *The Autobiography of Benjamin Franklin*, *Oedipus Rex*, and *The Old Man and the Sea* are banned from a state school curriculum.

A judge presiding over a lawsuit brought against the United Farm Workers chastised a witness for the farmers who had used the expression "for God's sake!" "I will not tolerate blasphemous language in this court," he warned. Later in his private chambers, he told the following joke: "Do you know how to make a Mexican omelet? Well, first you have to go out and steal three eggs...."

Jesus preached repentance.

We all need it. We have all rejected the dream of God, a good creation of a friendly world of friendly folk beneath a friendly sky. "We have each gone our own way, and the Lord has laid on him the iniquity of us all." We hear that verse from Second Isaiah as foreshadowing the suffering and death of Jesus, but of course the poet who wrote it meant no such thing. He was envisioning a saving people, a people who would live out before the world a new possibility for human life. The light of that community would change the world and bring the world nearer to God's dream.

I think the biblical name for God's dream is the kingdom of God. That was the central thrust of Jesus' ministry, and Mark's gospel shows Jesus beginning his ministry with the announcement that the kingdom of God is at hand.

Now when most people hear about the kingdom of God, they start thinking about pearly gates and streets of gold, with some of us getting there and some of us not. My sister had a little reading group once who would invite a learned professor in to discuss some theological issue. One time the topic was how various religions dealt with the concept of endtime, final things, eschatology. One member of the group, becoming impatient with all the polysyllabic words, announced, "You meet your mother in the skies. That's what it's all about—meeting your mother in the skies."

The professor was startled, and so, I believe, would Jesus have been. When Jesus talked about the kingdom of God, he meant the sovereignty of God, absolute allegiance to God, no other gods before the one God.

Jesus was thirty years old when he began his ministry, and he had spent those thirty years in a small village. We know nothing of those years except one glimpse in the gospel according to Luke, which reports a visit to the Temple when Jesus was twelve years old, already well versed in the scriptures of his people and eager to learn more.

Church folk have had many learned arguments about the exact time Jesus came to understand his vocation. Was it at his baptism, or did he know it before? I do not think the question is important. I certainly do not think we can answer it, because the earliest records were not interested in the question. They accepted Jesus as the expected Messiah and left psychologizing to our more sophisticated age. But the church loved the discussion because every argument you could spin out gave you a breathing space from decision.

The birth stories of Matthew and Luke are very beautiful poetry and that is what I think they are—the church singing its faith—but they are not essential to the witness. The earliest gospel does not have these stories of Jesus' birth, nor does the apostle Paul, who was the first to write about it. I remember talking with a group of Christian educators about the vignette in the gospels in which Mary goes with Jesus' brothers to call him home because they thought he was not quite all right, and one of the women asked earnestly, "Why would Mary do that? She knew all about the shepherds and the magi."

When I suggested those stories were not of the same stuff of history as the crucifixion, she was appalled. "What will I tell my children at Christmas?" she cried.

"Tell them about stars and angels and a baby born in Bethlehem," I said, "and live out for them the rest of the year that God is with them—Emmanuel." She is a wonderful Christian, and we are good friends, even yet.

So whatever happened to Jesus before he was thirty, at thirty he was baptized by John the Baptizer. And that was no insignificant decision.

It was a troubled time, and there were many solutions for the troubles. The Pharisees said, "Withdraw. Separate yourselves from the world." The very word Pharisee means "the separated ones." They withdrew into a life of holiness above the struggle, exerting their influence through the fostering of education and synagogue worship. The Pharisees were very open to interpretations of the Mosaic law and acquired quite a following among the common people because of their austerity and their hatred of the pagan rulers.

In contrast to the Pharisees were the Sadducees, whose answer was, "Cooperate." They represented the priestly aristocracy and the rich. Their strategy was to hold fast to the law as it was given by Moses, and in political matters they never rocked the boat.

The Zealots cried, "Revolt!" They agreed in all things with the Pharisees, but were attached to their liberty above all else and called God their only ruler and lord. They did not stop at achieving their ends by assassination.

A fourth solution was presented by the Essenes, a rigorous sect we have learned about from the Dead Sea Scrolls. Their solution was, "Deny the world." They lived a highly organized communistic life of monastic-like piety, abstaining from all but the simplest forms of earning their livelihood.

And then there was John the Baptist. His message was, "Repent!" John was a strange and fearsome character. He was clothed with camel's hair and had a leather girdle around his waist and ate locusts and wild honey— the very incarnation of an Old Testament prophet. He preached a fiery message and practiced a ritual cleansing. His program, however, was simple and direct. To the multitudes, which included Pharisees and Sadducees, he said, "He who has two coats, let him share with him who has none; and he who has food, let him do likewise." To the tax collectors, he said, "Collect no more than is appointed you." To the soldiers, he said, "Rob no one by violence or by false accusation, and be content with your wages."

Jesus cast his lot with John, and was baptized by him.

Church theologians have spent much time and paper wondering why Jesus was baptized. It was a baptism for repentance, and Jesus had nothing to repent, the argument goes, so why...? And so on, far, far into the night.

Once again, I think it is a non-issue. The early church had to wrestle with it, however, because the followers of John forced them to. John's followers were still on the scene after the death of Jesus and the birth of the Christian church; as the ambiguous witness of the gospels attests, the rivalry between the two groups was very strong. It may have been the case that after John's death, his followers made up a separate Jewish sect apart from

THE PERSISTENCE OF THE DREAM

the Christian church. Luke 3:15 records that there was
much speculation as to whether John might not be the
Christ. In Matthew 9:14 the disciples of John come to
Jesus, saying, "Why do we and the Pharisees fast, but your
disciples do not fast?" In Luke 11:2 Jesus' disciples ask
Jesus to teach them to pray because John taught his own
to pray.

Obviously, the followers of John were claiming that
their man was more important than the Christians' man
because John had baptized Jesus, so the Christians dealt
with that charge in their record. Mark's gospel says simply that Jesus came from Nazareth of Galilee and was
baptized by John in the Jordan. Matthew's later account
has John protest that he needs to be baptized by Jesus,
and Jesus replies in true Matthean style, "Let it be so
now; for thus it is fitting for us to fulfil all righteousness"
(3:15). In Luke, the people wonder if John is the Christ,
but he says, "Oh no, he who is mightier than I is coming," and Luke avoids specific mention that Jesus was
baptized by John (3:21). In the gospel according to John,
the Baptizer hails Jesus as "the Lamb of God, who takes
away the sin of the world" (1:29). John's gospel even
objectifies the confirmation of Jesus' mission, for the
Baptizer sees the Spirit descend on Jesus. In the other
accounts this experience of the heavens opening, the
dove descending, and the voice calling him the Beloved
Son is Jesus' alone.

The most important thing about Jesus' baptism is that
by it his mission is set. He is to show the world what it
means to live in the kingdom of his father, to live out
God's dream.

How will he do this?

That is what the temptation stories are about, dramatic episodes that show us Jesus testing alternative ways of doing what God would have him do.

The first possibility, of course, was good deeds. Feed the hungry. This is the first temptation in Matthew and Luke. The tempter's proposal is sound; that is the crux of temptation. It is attractive and reasonable and always has its good side. That is why it is a temptation. Something wholly bad does not tempt us.

And so there could not have been a better temptation. Jesus was hungry after forty days of fasting. He was keenly aware of the hunger and deprivation of his people. You want to show people that life can be different? Feed them. It is important with this story to remember it was a hungry man who resisted it, a hungry man who said, "Man shall not live by bread alone." An African proverb wisely says, "Full belly child cannot say to empty belly child, 'Be of good cheer.' Only empty belly child can say to empty belly child, 'Be of good cheer.'"

T. S. Eliot and St. Paul before him understood the flaw in good deeds. Eliot wrote in *Murder in the Cathedral* that the greatest treason is "to do the right deed for the wrong reason." St. Paul wrote, "If I give away all I have...but have not love, I gain nothing." Think of all the motives for doing good deeds that do not even take the other into account, such as good feelings (how we demean the poor!), credit in heaven (someone up there is keeping records), income tax break (keeping up with the Joneses)—that's my list. What's yours?

Jesus would not absolutize good deeds. There is one absolute—God.

The record shows that he did feed the hungry and his motivation was compassion, identification with their suffering. Compassion may take many forms. Some are called to minister in the soup kitchens. Some are called to challenge the systems that cause people to be hungry in a land of plenty.

The second temptation is power. In Luke's account, the devil shows Jesus all the kingdoms of the world and the power of them, and says it all belongs to him. I find that one of the most chilling lines in scripture. The kingdoms of this world and all the glory of them belong to the devil, and scripture knows the devil can speak the truth!

Power is the ability to get things done. Jesus did not give up power. He resisted power in the service of anyone other than God. "'You shall worship the Lord your God, and him only shall you serve.'"

Blacks and women have been powerless for so long that we have romanticized power. We imagine we will do better things with it than the white men have done, but it is part of this temptation to assume we will use power to good ends. Power corrupts, said Lord Acton, and absolute power corrupts absolutely. It must always recognize a limitation on itself. Power must always be in the service of the One from whom all power comes and under the judgment of God.

"My kingdom is not of this world," the early church remembered Jesus as having said. The later church immediately spiritualized the saying by setting the downtrodden to meditate on the sweet by-and-by, while those whose kingdoms were unabashedly of this world trod them down some more. Of course what Jesus meant was, "'My kingdom is not *like* the kingdoms of the world,'" and he tried to explain to his disciples what this kingdom was like. After three years with him, they still hadn't got the point.

> You know that those who are supposed to rule over the Gentiles lord it over them, and their great men exercise authority over them. But it shall not be so among you; but whoever would be great among you must be your servant, and whoever would be first among you must be slave of all. (Mark 10:42–44)

This is another understanding of power. It doesn't play well in Peoria, as they say—or in the church.

Luke's third temptation, I think, is the most subtle of all. It combines the first two—the temptation to do good deeds and the temptation to exercise power come together in the temptation to profit from being religious. Notice that the scene is a church. The devil took Jesus to the pinnacle of the Temple and said, "If you are the Son of God, throw yourself down from here; for it is written, 'He will give his angels charge over you, to guard you' and 'On their hands they will bear you up, lest you strike your foot against a stone'" (Luke 4:9–10).

By this time Jesus must have been very weary of this incessant questioning of his vocation, especially as the devil prefaced all the temptations with the subtle "If—?" By this time Jesus must have been almost at the point of saying, "I'll show you! I'll throw myself down. I'll show you I'm special."

And there's the rub. We want to be special, and we want everybody to know it. Not to God's glory, but to ours.

How the heresy that if you are virtuous and one of God's chosen, you will escape all the ills of the flesh has prospered in the church! "I've never seen the righteous forsaken or his seed begging bread," the minister of my childhood church used to intone. My father, wonderful skeptic that he was, used to observe, "It was a king who said that. The fact that he hadn't seen it didn't mean it hadn't happened."

It has always seemed to me an irony of Christianity that the one it calls its founder eschewed miracle as proof of his relationship with his Father, but the church has used the resurrection as miraculous proof of his divine sonship. The devil said, "Prove you are the Son of God by throwing yourself down from the pinnacle of the Temple and letting God rescue you." Jesus refused to do that, but the church has made his "bursting from the spiced tomb" the foundation stone of its theology.

Jesus himself always pointed to what he *did*. When John's disciples asked for his credentials, Jesus replied, "Go and tell John what you hear and see: the blind receive their sight and the lame walk, lepers are cleansed and the deaf hear, and the dead are raised up, and the poor have good news preached to them" (Matthew 11:4–5).

The resurrection remains the greatest mystery of all. It does not force us to have faith. God keeps God's part of the bargain to leave the free creature free.

I have always been moved by the mysterious ending to Mark's gospel. The women come to the tomb. They meet a young man who tells them Jesus is risen, and they are to let his disciples know he is going before them to Galilee. And the women flee from the tomb in fear.

That is the end of the first Easter story.

Why were they afraid? I think they understood that Jesus had rightly divined the mind of the Father as to the cost of the good creation. They, too, would have to face the decision to follow him—with all its cost—or abandon him—with all the cost of that. It is a decision to make one very much afraid.

I think Jesus left his temptation experience with his mind made up as to the way he would go, a way that would bring him into direct confrontation with the kingdoms of the world. His first act was to gather the new community around him—the second effort of God to create a people who would live out the kingdom of God in the presence of the kingdoms of the world. The little community itself was a witness to something new in the world. Matthew, the tax collector, with James and John, the faithful Jews. Judas Iscariot, the Zealot, with Peter, the conservative. It took a matchless leader to hold that bunch together.

And he taught them. That is what the title rabbi means—teacher. He taught them in the ancient way, by telling them stories. Since then the stories have been changed and twisted and allegorized out of their original impact, but at the time Jesus told them, they were startling stories, confrontational stories, stories of another way of life. He told them stories about laborers who worked only an hour but earned as much as those who had borne the burden and heat of the day, and stories of a scalawag younger son who had wasted his father's inheritance in the far country but had a party thrown for him when desperation drove him back. He went on telling stories, all kinds of stories, always ending with the question, "And what would you do?"

Despite the gathering storm, Jesus knew he must go to Jerusalem and confront the religious and political powers at the seat of their power. On the road he asked, "Who do people say that I am?" Peter, with obviously little idea of what he was talking about, told him, "You are the Christ." Christ is the Greek word for the Hebrew Messiah, the one by whom the kingdom of God will be made known.

Then Jesus told them what must happen to the Messiah. He will confront the kingdoms of this world and be destroyed by them, wresting his victory out of that defeat.

Peter was appalled. "This can't happen to you!" he cried. Jesus was once again back in temptation's hour, once again hearing that insidious voice, "I have an easier way!" Give the people what they most desperately want. Give the people the security of power. Give the people the comfort of the miraculous.

"Get behind me, Satan!" he cried.

But that was not the end of it. Peter had heard nothing of the victory, while James and John had heard nothing of the defeat. They foresaw a victory parade—an inauguration—and they wanted to be sure they had the places of honor. "When you come into your glory, Jesus," they asked, "let us sit on your right hand and on your left."

Jesus called the little band about him and explained once again what life in the kingdom of God is like. It is not like life in the kingdoms of this world. We have a new vision. We are called to a new ministry, even as "the Son of man also came not to be served but to serve." St. Paul picked that up in his second letter to the Corinthian church:

> Therefore, if any one is in Christ, he is a new creation; the old has passed away, behold, the new has come. All this is from God, who through Christ reconciled us to himself and gave us the ministry of reconciliation.... So we are ambassadors for Christ, God making his appeal through us. (2 Corinthians 5:17–20a)

The word the translators put into the mouth of Jesus—
serve—and the word attributed to St. Paul—*ministry*—
are the same.

The call to ministry is the call to be a citizen of the
kingdom of God in a new way, the daring, free, accept-
ing, compassionate way Jesus modeled. It means being
bound by no yesterday, fearing no tomorrow, drawing no
lines between friend and foe, the acceptable ones and the
outcasts. Ministry is commitment to the dream of God.

The world is not as God would have it be. The kingdoms
of this world are not yet the kingdom of God, but they
can become it. They are not yet the realm where God's
sovereignty is acknowledged and lived out, but they can
become it.

I think we have lost the capacity to dream great
dreams. We reduce God to the personal, private, "spiritual" sphere of our lives, and ministry to personal, private,
"spiritual" acts—a good deed here, a good deed there; a
cup of cold water here, a loaf of freshly baked bread there;
a prison visit here, a hospital call there; a night in a shelter here, a time with a troubled friend there. We see no
need to challenge the systems that make these "ministries" necessary. We see no need to value the small
Congressional committees that work for the nation's
health, the nation's children, or the nation's small entre-
preneurs, to see the fallen world as a field "white unto
harvest." We have no need to see ministry as more than
merely the special ones acting out of the abundance of
the grace that has been given to them.

But even that is a step forward. Back when I first start-
ed talking about ministry, it was seen as something the

ordained did. Lay people had no ministry at all except as they participated in the work of the institution. If you taught in the Christian education program, you had a ministry. If you taught in the public schools, you "did time" five days a week until you could get to your ministry. When I began my second career, people would say to me, "You taught school for thirty-two years; then you began your ministry." In my unredeemed way, I would steel myself and reply through clenched teeth, "No, I *continued* my ministry!"

Jesus was a carpenter for two decades, and I wager the yokes he made rested like a blessing on the oxen and inspired his invitation, "Take my yoke upon you, and learn from me; . . . for my yoke is easy." It was a lesson his apostles found hard to learn, and they made a bad response to the problems caused by their evangelistic success. Very soon one group was complaining that their folks were being overlooked by another group in the distribution of food, so the Twelve decided to organize things better by introducing an unfortunate division of labor:

> It is not right that we should give up preaching the word of God to serve tables. Therefore, brethren, pick out from among you seven men of good repute, full of the Spirit and of wisdom, whom we may appoint to this duty. But we will devote ourselves to prayer and to the ministry of the word. (Acts 6:2–4)

The seeds were sown for the exaltation of preaching and praying over cooking and serving—and this from men whose feet had been washed by their Lord!

The decision was a serious flaw that marred the development of the church as it evolved more and more into an institution down through the ages, becoming less and less the people of God. The *laos*, the people of God, was divided into two groups—the clergy and the laity—the learned and the ignorant, the holy and the hangers-on, the controlling and the controlled. Such was the post-biblical church, such was the church of the Middle Ages, and so it has continued to this day.

But the sleeping giant is stirring. Clergy and laity are beginning to realize that the kingdom of God will never become the reality God dreamed as long as part of the *laos* struggles to maintain an institution, while the other part drops by on holy days to participate in an archaic ritual that has no effect on the lives they are leading the rest of the time.

The church is the people of God. It takes two forms, the church gathered and the church scattered. We gather to break bread as a community, to hear our story, and to recommit ourselves to the dream of God. We scatter to live into that dream.

It is the task of the church, the people of God, to minister within the structures of society. It is the role of the church, the institution, to support that ministry.

The people of God with kingdom-of-God ideas about money need to work in the financial and economic structures of our society. Decisions about how money is earned, shared, spent, and invested are not to be surrendered to the kingdoms of the world. The statement "Render therefore to Caesar the things that are Caesar's, and to God the things that are God's" does not mean the world is divided into sacred and secular, but that priorities have to be established. Someone has said that if you render unto God the things that are God's, there will be little left to render unto Caesar. To call Jesus "Lord" is to say Caesar is not. The early Christians understood that.

The people of God with kingdom-of-God ideas about power need to work in the political structures of our world, the governments of town and city, state and nation. People who know a way other than the way of domination and oppression, people who can risk the power of powerlessness, the vulnerability of God.

The people of God with kingdom-of-God ideas about prestige need to work in all the structures of society that serve others. How often the marginalized are demeaned by the very people whose business it is to serve them! How many teachers dislike students, how many social workers despise the poor, how many parents have contempt for the young. Contempt is manifested in many ways, overt and subtle.

The people of God with kingdom-of-God ideas about human solidarity need to be in all the structures of society where people find meaning—in the arts, in journalism, in universities, in city planning, in the sciences. There is no place where the people of God should not be, and wherever they are they are called to witness to another possibility for life.

That is ministry, being about God's business. Ministry is participating in God's dream of a good creation, and Jesus is the model.

Do you want to follow Jesus? Or are you content just to worship him, and postpone for just a little longer the fulfillment of the dream of God?

Questions immediately arise. "How do you follow Jesus?" "What would following Jesus look like?" We are always asking for prescriptions. We want to be safe, to be sure we are doing the right thing. That to me is the voice of the Tempter.

Kingdom-of-God thinking calls us to risk. We always see through a glass darkly, and that is what faith is about. I will live by the best I can discern today. Tomorrow I may find out I was wrong. Since I do not live by being right, I am not destroyed by being wrong. The God revealed in Jesus whom I call the Christ is a God whose forgiveness goes ahead of me, and whose love sustains me and the whole created world. That God bursts all the definitions of our small minds, all the limitations of our timid efforts, all the boundaries of our institutions.

As I was writing this, there arrived in the mail a church newsletter from a friend. It contained the transcript of a recent sermon on Matthew 9:35–10:15, the calling and sending out of the Twelve.

> The Lord's resurrection power is available to us, as to the twelve. We discover that availability as we use it, as we exercise his ministry. It is never clear ahead of time that we can or will be able to do whatever is appropriate. In fact, in and of ourselves, we probably don't have what it takes. The powerful love of Jesus is never something we possess. Only by going out in faith, often with fear and trembling, do we rediscover the truth. As today's lesson indicates, he gives power and authority to his disciples, when they are about his ministry. Whatever is needed is somehow provided, in the moment. To one and all. All of us are called to come to Jesus—which means to learn more about his love. And all of us are called to share in his outreaching ministry of compassion for those in need. Jumping in is always a leap of faith, every time.

Nothing scares us more than freedom. We are always afraid that freedom will degenerate into chaos—as it often does—so to escape chaos we flee to authority, which means authoritarianism.

The urgent task for us today is to reclaim our identity as the people of God and live into our high calling as the baptized community. We are a chosen people, chosen for God's high purposes, that the dream of God for a new

creation may be realized. God has paid us the high compliment of calling us to be coworkers with our Creator, a
compliment so awesome that we have fled from it and
taken refuge in the church. God does not need such an
institution. "Destroy this temple," Jesus said, "and I will
rebuild it in three days."

The institution is replaceable. The living body of
God's people is not.

Like Esau, we have surrendered our birthright.

The institution is the servant of the people, but it has
presumed to become the master. When oppressed people
have struggled to find new ways to make the ancient heritage alive once more, with base communities or worker
priests, the institution has shaken its bony finger in their
faces and scolded them as if they were naughty children.

"Behold, I make all things new" is the word of the
Lord, but the institution damns newness as novelty or
trend, and herds the sheep back to the security of the old
fold. Jesus said, "You have heard it said of old, but behold,
I say unto you...." Yet the institution claims the Bible
says only one thing, and only the church can interpret it.

We the people are responsible for what the institution
has done. We have allowed God's gracious gift to us of
order, continuity, and memory to become a monster of
control, irrelevance, and idolatry. To paraphrase the old
gospel spiritual, it's nobody's fault but ours.

The institution has preserved the biblical record in all
its ambiguity—all the sacred writings, all the ancient
struggles, all the history down to this present hour. We
can study it and see for ourselves that at no time was the
vision clear and unambiguous. From the time of its birth
as a people, Israel *interpreted* its history and then transmitted it in oral and written tradition as an expression of
life in fellowship with God, in response to God's call,
God's promises, and God's commandments. The inter-

pretation of history as the expression of a divine-human relationship runs throughout scripture.

Faith never says, "This is how it was," but, "This is how we saw it." Faith always includes the possibility it could at any given moment be wrong, and that is why it requires courage. Faith is taking the risk that what I understand today calls for commitment of heart and mind and soul, even though at all times I know that what I understand today may be revealed to be wanting tomorrow.

What I understand about God is not God. Even Jesus was understood to be the fullness of the Godhead *bodily*, not the fullness of the Godhead. Jesus was not God. That is a paradox the institution dare not wrestle with because it can purvey only certainties. We are faithless people who demand certainties. The institution, the faithless shepherd, doles out certainties to us and is rewarded with our unquestioning allegiance.

O what a tangled web we have woven! How do we begin to untangle it?

The first step, I believe, is to demystify the institution, to set it in its proper place as the servant of the people of God.

Let us look unflinchingly at the slippery road we have traveled since the time of Jesus of Nazareth. Since then we have divided the people of God into two groups. The division was not in itself bad, because a division of labor is necessary to get a body functioning. Hands cannot see. Eyes cannot walk. The separation of the body into clergy and laity was not intrinsically sinful; it did not of itself mean that we missed the mark of God's high calling to share in the fulfillment of the dream. The sin lay in what we did with the division, assigning to one part the designation that belonged to the whole people of God—holiness. Baptism was no longer all that was necessary to identify the chosen. We had to pile on ordinations and consecrations to mark the especially chosen. All were equal, but some were more equal than others.

All the people of God are called, but somehow the vocation to ordained ministry became a calling to a special ministry, a ministry set apart. Set apart for what? We never did the hard work to answer that question.

Volumes have been written on ministry, but if any of them defined the clergy as a part of the people of God with a work to do for the whole people, which was no more or no less important than any other kind of ministry, this fact never filtered down to the laity. Even the word "ministry" was taken over by one part of the people. Ministry was the calling of the clergy; lay people could only aspire to lay ministry, a second-class ministry of helping the clergy.

Ministry was the high calling of Jesus of Nazareth. It is one way of translating *diakonia*, service. Jesus came to serve the world, to restore it to the oneness with God from which it had fallen. That restoration—"reconciliation" is the word St. Paul used—is always the mission of the people of God. Any talk about ministry that does not talk about reconciliation has already missed the mark.

Ministry is serving the world God loves. The people of God are sent to love the world—the *people* of the world, not the kingdoms of the world, not the way of life that exalts one person over another, greed over giving, power over vulnerability, the kingdoms of this world over against the kingdom of God. Jesus made the choice for the kingdom of God, the choice that led him to the cross.

One of the bitterest choices the people of God have made is trying to have both the kingdoms of this world and the kingdom of God. One way is to live with the distortions the church has imposed on the *laos*, the people of God.

We have been comfortable living with these distortions because they have allowed us to feast at the tables of the empire six days a week and then bow down to archaic rituals the seventh day as a kind of death insurance, in case there really is a sweet by-and-by. Meanwhile, the institution got the money to build its church buildings and carry on its increasingly elaborate and irrelevant fantasies.

The people of God are called to a possibility other than the kingdoms of the world. They must be ambassadors—again, St. Paul's word—in every part of life. They witness to another way that governments can relate to one another, that money can be earned and spent, that doctors and caregivers and engineers and lawyers and teachers can serve their constituencies, that wordsmiths and musicians and artists and philosophers can give us new visions of the human condition. That is the ministry of the laity.

All of them need the support system of the institutional church. There must be those resting places where the story is treasured and passed on in liturgy and education. There must be those islands of refuge where the wounded find healing; the confused, light; the fearful, courage; the lonely, community; the alienated, acceptance; the strong, gratitude. Maintaining such institutions is the ministry of the clergy.

We have all failed the dream of God. The terribly patient God still waits.

1. Henry Mitchell, "Spiritual Revival, 1980s Style," *The Washington Post* (June 10, 1988).
2. Will Campbell, *The Florida Times-Union / Jacksonville Journal* (May 2, 1988).

DISCUSSION QUESTIONS AND EXTRA RESOURCES FOR *THE DREAM OF GOD*

Written by The Very Rev. Robyn Szoke-Coolidge, Dean, the Stevenson School for Ministry, and Mary Novello, Vice President, Commission on Ministry, Episcopal Diocese of Central Pennsylvania

A word from the developers of the study guide: Beginning in 2018, the Episcopal Diocese of Central Pennsylvania's Commission on Ministry has been working to widen its focus from ordained ministry to the ministry of all baptized people. Although the importance of baptismal ministry is clearly spelled out in the Book of Common Prayer, we discovered that, as a diocese, we all had a lot to learn. The COVID pandemic provided us with an opportunity to explore online learning open to the entire diocese. Using Facebook Live Streaming, with Zoom-linked hosts and occasional prerecorded video, we hoped to reach as many people as possible to take a deep dive into Verna Dozier's *The Dream of God*, a down-to-earth approach exhorting laypeople to claim their authority, their ministry, and get busy restoring the Dream of God. We followed a conversational approach, using as many lay leaders as possible, as we attempted to build a common frame of reference and theological vocabulary regarding discernment and ministry for all God's people.

Using this study guide: You may use this guide with a small parish-based group, with a diocesan Commission on Ministry–based cohort, or for individual study. Throughout the study, hear Verna asking: "What does this mean for your ministry?"

QUESTIONS TO EXPLORE BY CHAPTER

CHAPTER 1

- From your understanding of scripture, how would you describe the dream of God? In the dream of God, what are people called to?
- Why do you believe people reject the dream of God?
- Reflect and share how you read the Bible and what the biblical passages and stories mean to you.

CHAPTER 2

- The act of Creation is a love story in which the lover (God) seeks the beloved (us) in a way that God is made vulnerable and is painted as "lonely." *How do you respond to the idea of a vulnerable, lonely God?*
- God creates humankind as "free." *How does your freedom play into your relationship with God? How have you rejected or lived into God's idea of a "friendly world or friendly folk under a friendly sky"? How does this differ from the popular idea that "God has a plan for your life"?*
- God's dream is of a restored world in which God's people live in a covenant relationship with God. We see the cycle of wandering, sin, wailing, repentance, restoration, wandering, sin, wailing, repentance. . . . *Where do you think we are right now, as a people, as a country?*
- Jesus' life and ministry is shared in scripture in four different gospel accounts (the various vantages are described on pp. 36 and 37). *Which one resonates most with you?*

116

CHAPTER 3

- The important question to ask is not "What do you believe?" but "What difference does it make that you believe?" (p. 105).

- The sovereignty of the reign of God and the kingdom of God are theological symbols for a possibility to be realized, a possibility never to be realized. It is realized eschatology: the kingdom is here; the kingdom is still to come. It is a faith statement about the dream of God. *How do the ministries you or your congregations are involved in reveal the dream of God?*

- The church is first of all a people called to live out this statement. Jesus infused his followers with his spirit that even when he died, they knew he lived. That movement swept on in power until it could no longer trust in the uncertainty of God. *Where do you see the church engaging in the uncertainty of God and in tension with the institutional church?*

CHAPTER 4

- Do you want to follow Jesus, or are you content just to worship him (p. 143)?

- Jesus called people to follow him, not worship him. We worship God. *What difference does it make that you believe?*

- *What does the church do with Jesus?* Are we in the power of the Kingdom come rather than living in an expectation of a beyond-time event? Jesus is both the present and the future.

- *Why does the church turn Jesus into a miracle to be revered instead of simply following Jesus, who took action during the temptations by rejecting carrying out his mission by miracle (turning stones into bread) and by exercising power (responding to the kingdoms of this world)? What does it mean to follow Jesus or join the Jesus Movement?*

- Jesus was lifted up by God after he died, which gave him a new kind of life, where he could be present to any disciple anywhere. *The question is not what happened in the tomb but "What is God about to do?"*

- Ray Brown, in *The Churches the Apostles Left Behind*, states, "The great anomaly of Christianity is that only through an institution can the message of a non-institutional Jesus be preserved." *How do you believe the message of Jesus is not being altered to fit the needs of the institution? Or, how do you believe the message of Jesus is being altered to fit the needs of the institution?*

- Respond to the quote from William Clebsch, one of the young radicals who founded the Episcopal Seminary of the Southwest in Austin, Texas. He warned that "faith in order to be incarnate must risk becoming a religion, but religion is always in danger of murdering faith."

- *What have we not listened to in the Bible? What needs our attention for now?*

CHAPTER 5

- The genius of Christianity is the vision of a new possibility for human life rooted in an ancient understanding of God that Jesus articulated. *Where have we rejected the dream of God? Or the kingdom of God?*

- Baptism is to show the world what it means to live in the kingdom of God, to live out God's dream. Not absolutizing good deeds—there is one absolute and that is God. Jesus resisted power in the service of anyone other than God. The temptation to do good deeds and to exercise power in the temptation is to profit from being religious. *How does the present church profit from being religious? And what would it look like if only God were being served? Do we struggle to save the institution or to live the life of the kingdom of God, the Church gathered, the church scattered?*

- The third temptation of Jesus in the wilderness was at the church, the pinnacle of the temple, confronting the kingdoms of the world. "There is no place that the kingdom of God should not be, and wherever they are . . . they are called to witness to another possibility for life. . . ." *Do you want to follow Jesus or are you content just to worship him?*

- The church as the servant of the people of God is found in the mission of the people of God. We must talk about reconciliation and witness to another way; a new vision of the human condition. This is the ministry of the laity. *What does this mean for your ministry?*

- Does the world come nearer to the dream of God because of what you believe?

POSSIBLE MULTIMEDIA RESOURCES

INTRODUCTION TO VERNA DOZIER: AN ONLINE SEARCH

"Verna Dozier: Steps of the Faithful with KD Johnson": *https://www.youtube.com/watch?v=O9UFxGJgtwY.* Learning about Verna Dozier to be inspired.

"Verna Dozier: World": *https://www.youtube.com/watch?v= 0giAg2qP9mY.* Video clip about dominion.

"My Story | Social Justice: Verna Dozier": *www.youtube. com/watch?v=zlj01j1335w.* St. Michael and All Angel's, Dallas: My Story series about Dozier—how are we living out our story in everyday life?

"Living Courageously in Times like These": *https://www.facebook.com/Education.for.Ministry/videos/156 9717103041338*. Frederica Harris Thomestt on Verna Dozier, after-dinner speech at EfM retreat. At 19:06, an exercise Dr. Dozier gave at a College of Preachers program. Summary: Tell the story of the Bible in one paragraph. Well-known preachers struggled with it. She did it in five words: Created, Chosen, Sent, Forgiven, and Pursued.

"Verna Josephine Dozier" by Fredrica Harris Thomsett: *https://www.biola.edu/talbot/ce20/database/verna-josephine-dozier*. Biola University, Christian Educators.

"Verna Dozier, 1917–2006": *https://episcopalarchives.org/church-awakens/exhibits/show/leadership/lay/dozier*. Episcopal Church Leadership Gallery.

CPSIA information can be obtained
at www.ICGtesting.com
Printed in the USA
JSHW040010210322
24074JS00004B/4